Played in Birmingham

Charting the heritage of a city at play

Played in Birmingham
© English Heritage 2006

English Heritage
is the government's statutory
advisor on all aspects of the
historic environment

112 Colmore Row
Birmingham B3 3AG
www.english-heritage.org.uk

Design by Doug Cheeseman

Production by Jackie Spreckley
Additional Imaging by Jörn Kröger
Maps by Mark Fenton
For image credits see page 150

Malavan Media is a creative
consultancy responsible
for the Played in Britain series
www.playedinbritain.co.uk

Printed by Zrinski, Croatia
ISBN: 0 954744 519
Product code: 51079

Played in Birmingham

Charting the heritage of a city at play

Steve Beauchampé & Simon Inglis

ENGLISH HERITAGE

Setting sail for London 2012? One of Birmingham's greatest recreational assets, and yet one of its least known too, is Edgbaston Reservoir, where the Midland Sailing Cub offers weekly training sessions for all ages. Formed in 1894 and one of the oldest of its type in inland Britain, the club has over 100 members and a fleet of some 60 boats in such classes as the Optimist (*shown here*), Topper, Feva, Enterprise, Solo, GP14 and Merlin Rocket. The reservoir itself, created in the 1820s, is only one of a surprisingly large number of waterscapes dotted around Birmingham. To fully appreciate its expanse, and its proximity to the city centre, see page 96.

Page Two Action from March 1960 at the much-loved Reddings ground, the homely home of Moseley Rugby Football Club for 120 years, but now an estate of executive houses and flats.

Page One International tennis at the Edgbaston Priory Club, in June 2005. This verdant district of the city may justly claim to have been the birthplace of lawn tennis during the 1860s, while the Priory club is one of the oldest in the world, having formed in 1875 and moved to its current, extensive, yet remarkably secluded site in the 1880s. A pavilion in its midst (*see page 117*) may well be the oldest sports building in Birmingham.

Contents

Foreword

Foreword

by Councillor Mike Whitby, Leader of Birmingham City Council

As a former athlete myself, I have a special interest in sport, and am particularly proud of Birmingham's international reputation for staging highly successful sporting events.

Our city has staged no fewer than 23 World, and 11 European major sporting championships since 1991, more than any other British city.

Among them have been the World Disability Athletics Championships in 1998 and the World Indoor Athletics Championships in 2003.

These last championships, which attracted over 4,000 athletes and officials from 143 countries, plus 1,000 media representatives, were described by the President of the IAAF (the International Association of Athletics Federations) as 'the best ever'.

Former IAAF General Secretary Istvan Guylai added, 'I have seen all World Athletics Championships, and never before have I witnessed more support from the host city.'

Accolades indeed and a reflection, not only of the depth of expertise that exists within the city for organizing major public and sporting events, but also of the passion of Birmingham people for sport.

At a crucial time in the build up to London's bid for the 2012 Olympics, our staging of the 2003 championships was also widely credited with restoring confidence in the country's ability to host major sporting events.

We in Birmingham already feel a part of the UK team aiming to deliver an inspirational Olympic and Paralympic Games for 2012, and have set up a task force specifically to maximise the benefits to Birmingham and its people, not just in economic terms but by harnessing the power such events have to inspire young people to make sport a central part of their lives.

We are also looking at building on our own excellent track record in staging major sports events. For example, we are actively assessing the feasibility of a future bid for a Commonwealth Games.

As this beautifully illustrated and informative book shows, Birmingham has a rich and fascinating sporting heritage.

Birmingham was the cradle of League Football in the 1880s. The Edgbaston Archery and Lawn Tennis Society can claim to be the oldest lawn tennis club in the world. Following on from the pioneering efforts of the Cadbury brothers at Bournville, the city's industrial companies led the way in their provision of sports facilities for working people.

This book will also surprise many readers by showing just how much green space there is for recreation in the city, and how much water too.

I am therefore delighted that our sponsorship of this, the latest in English Heritage's *Played in Britain* series, will help to raise awareness of Birmingham's wonderful sporting heritage to a wider audience.

If you live in the region, I am certain the book will make you even more proud of Birmingham.

And if you are visiting, I hope it will give you an even greater incentive to explore further, and to enjoy this great city of ours.

The passion and enthusiasm shown by Birmingham crowds attending such events as the Norwich Union Grand Prix at the National Indoor Arena has been widely noted by international sporting bodies. Since opening in 1991, in addition to athletics the arena has staged Davis Cup tennis, badminton, basketball, judo, powerlifting, table tennis and wrestling.

◀ Sporting weathervanes adorn the clubhouse of **Handsworth Golf Club** (*top*) and the 1950s swimming pool at **Kings Edward's School**, Edgbaston (*below left*).

Less expected is this replica (*below right*) of the famous Old Father Time weathervane at Lord's Cricket Ground in London. Spotted in the garden of a house in Harborne, the replica was a gift to a much admired cricket master from staff and pupils at Queensbridge School, Moseley.

Chapter One

Played in Birmingham

An artfully weathered pavilion at a typical suburban sports ground – that of the Bishop Challoner School, on Moor Green Lane, Moseley. The question is, where do we draw the line between a building that appears decorative and quaint, and one that is significant in terms of sporting heritage? And although dozens of pattern-book, timber-framed pavilions like this are dotted around Birmingham, there will come a time when only a handful remain. So is this a shed, or a relic of popular culture? *Played in Birmingham*, it is hoped, will help readers to decide.

There are numerous ways of understanding and defining a great metropolis: by examining its history, its people, its geography and built environment, its industry and economy, and not least its self-image and aspirations.

Played in Birmingham seeks to study, celebrate and reflect all these characteristics through the medium of sport.

In doing so, our aim is to develop an appreciation of which sports-related buildings and 'sportscapes' – that is, landscapes and waterscapes used for sport – are of significance, in social, architectural and historical terms.

Because *Played in Birmingham* is part of the wider *Played in Britain* study being carried out on behalf of English Heritage, its remit is also to assess the city's sporting heritage in relation to national, and even international, criteria.

The book is divided into four sections. Following this chapter's summary of sporting development in the Birmingham area, we study five areas; Edgbaston, Bournville, the Tame Valley, Sutton Park and Moor Pool Estate, Harborne. Each

area has been selected because it contains a 'cluster' of sportscapes, whose ownership, origins and patterns of usage share common roots, or whose development illustrates common themes. Most cities have such clusters. Finding out how and why they came about can provide useful insights into a city's character.

Next are four thematic chapters, taking a city-wide look at specific types of buildings and sportscapes. These are followed by a chapter on the manufacture of sporting goods.

The remaining chapters focus on individual sports, our choice of which might seem idiosyncratic. There are no individual studies of football or cricket, for example. Instead, we focus on those sports and recreations whose legacy is perhaps less well understood or appreciated, or that, as in the case of bowls and swimming, have made a special contribution to Birmingham's historic environment.

As the map on page 17 shows, the scope of our study extends marginally beyond the city of

Birmingham's boundaries, into parts of Sandwell and Solihull. However, any significant West Midlands, Worcestershire or Warwickshire examples that lie beyond this book's scope will, it is intended, be covered in future thematic studies being prepared as part of the series (*see Links*).

Pre-Victorian 'sport'

There is a common view that sport as we know it today is essentially a Victorian construct.

This is not wholly accurate. But it is the case that until the mid 19th century the term 'sport' generally referred to bloodsports or so-called 'cruel sports', and also to any form of gambling associated with such activities such as cock-fighting and horse racing.

Of all these, the earliest recorded in the study area is hunting, starting in the 12th century with landscaped deer parks both in Sutton and in the area now forming Birmingham city centre, where excavations have revealed the existence of ditches underneath Selfridges, Moor Street and Park Street. Such

Joseph Strutt sums up the *Played in Britain* ethos in his seminal study of 1801, *The Sports and Pastimes of the People of England*.

In order to form a just estimation of the character of any particular people, it is absolutely necessary to investigate the Sports and Pastimes most generally prevalent among them.

ditches – traces of which can still be seen in Sutton Park – formed the boundaries of parks, to prevent deer from escaping.

In the 16th century another form of bloodsport arrived in the town, courtesy of one John Cooper. Baiting, a visceral blend of butchery and betting, required a bull, or bear, to be chained to a stake in the middle of a ring (hence the 'Bull Ring'). Specially bred dogs, such as Staffordshire bull terriers, were then incited to attack, the winner being the dog able to hang on the longest, usually by clamping its teeth onto the bull's nose.

It was an unedifying but wildly popular spectacle, described in *Aris's Gazette* (one of the town's first newspapers) in 1764 as 'a disgrace to real Christianity'. (Butchers claimed in response that the bull's meat tasted better if they were slaughtered after a baiting.)

Baiting was eventually banned from the marketplace in 1773, although it resurfaced at Snow Hill in 1786, where it met stiff resistance from a militia hired by the Birmingham Association, a body set up by concerned local traders. Thereafter, baiting moved beyond the militia's reach, to Handsworth, where it drew large crowds until being outlawed by the government in 1835.

Bloodsports enjoyed by the social elite survived rather longer. Deer hunting had ceased at Aston Park by the early 19th century, but the newly fashionable sport of fox hunting carried on at Four Oaks Park until the 1880s, and at Sutton Park, remarkably, until 1970.

Meanwhile, the first evidence of 'sport' in the modern sense of a game, relates to bowls. Played since at least the 13th century in other parts of the country, its

earliest confirmed arrival in the Birmingham area is at Aston Hall, where Sir Thomas Holte laid out a green c.1635. This was followed by a green at what is now The George Hotel, Solihull c.1693. Still in use today, the latter is probably the oldest sports ground extant in the area covered by this book.

However, the first record in the Birmingham area of organised sport – that is, with fixtures between recognised teams or representatives from different towns or counties – appears in the 1750s, primarily, as in other parts of the country, in the realm of cock-fighting and cricket.

The reason for this is that both these apparently contrasting 'sports' attracted widespread betting, which in turn required participants to adhere to an agreed set of rules. (From this it can be deduced that the British penchant for codifying sport, so prevalent in the 19th century, derived from a love of gambling as much as from any leanings towards fair play.)

Typical was a report in *Aris's Gazette* of a 'main' (or match) of 15 cocks per side being staged between the Gentlemen of Warwickshire and Worcestershire, on St Stephen's Day 1759, at The Red Lion, Moseley (later renamed The Fighting Cocks.) Another notice, in 1809, offered teams '£5 5s the battle, 100 guineas the main' at a 'new pit' established in Smallbrook Street.

But even before the scheduling of fixtures became commonplace, cockfighting had already been long established in the area. Documents from the 1690s, for example, refer to the existence of Cockpit Close, behind The Lamb Inn, in the area close to where construction of the new St Philip's Cathedral would commence in ➤➤

▲ Birmingham's first sporting pin-up was **Isaac Perrins** (1750–1800), seen here squaring up to Tom Johnson from Derby, at one of the most celebrated, and bloodiest ever bareknuckle prize fights, staged at Banbury on 22 October 1789.

Standing 6 foot 3 inches tall and weighing 17 stone, Perrins – a factory foreman and one-time choirmaster – was known as the Gentle Giant. A reluctant pugilist, he was apparently browbeaten into fighting by both his manager and his mother-in-law (known herself as 'Fighting Mac').

At the time of the Banbury encounter Perrins was aged 39 and undefeated. He and Johnson were to share a sizeable purse of 250 guineas each (approximately £50,000 today), a figure greatly increased by side bets. In the fight's early stages it appeared a non-contest, as Perrins derided the fancy footwork of his much smaller opponent. 'You have imposed on me a mere boy!' he was reported to have cried out, at which point an indignant Johnson sprang up and

closed Perrins' left eye with a fierce lunge. And so it continued for 62 rounds and 75 minutes, at the end of which Perrins had to be dragged from the ring by his seconds.

He never fought again, retiring instead to Manchester, where he died eleven years later after saving a woman and at least four children from a blaze.

But Perrins' reputation, and the fame of his final bout – 'the most severe battle ever seen' as once described – lived on. This engraving, by Joseph Grozer, was copied from an original by Conrad Martin Metz and re-issued 23 years after the event by a London publisher. The image was also sold in the form of medallions, and later turned into a rather romanticised oil painting by W Allen, now in the collection of Birmingham Museum and Art Gallery.

Another Birmingham pugilist was the Scottish-born Thomas Futrell – a pupil of Perrins and the winner of the first ever prize fight in Scotland – who squandered most of his substantial earnings on wagers.

▲ From the 1880s until 1914, Birmingham was Britain's leading centre for gymnastics, with the city's most advanced gymnasium being that of the **Birmingham Athletic Institute** on **John Bright Street**, designed by BR Corser and opened in 1892. Its resident club, the Birmingham Athletics Club (formed in 1866), trained Walter Tysall, the only British gymnast to have won an individual medal at the Olympics, having taken silver at the London games in 1908.

Other prominent clubs among the 138 formed in the Midlands between 1866 and 1917 included the YMCA, whose gym opened in Needless Alley in 1875, and the **Dolobran Athletic Club**, formed in 1884 at Christ Church, on Dolobran Road, Sparkbrook. By 1900 this club had grown so large, with approaching 700 members, that with help from club president Barrow Cadbury (son of Richard Cadbury) it set up a new gym at the Friends Institute on Moseley Road. It was there that the first

ever international gymnastics match staged in England, involving Scotland and Ireland, was held in March 1900. (A similar event held in Dublin the previous year had by chance been attended by Birmingham councillor William Adams, who donated a shield, still regarded as the most prized award in English men's gymnastics.)

In addition to competition, by holding regular public classes the BAC, YMCA and Dolobran played a key role in improving fitness levels in Birmingham, while at the same time training a whole generation of physical education instructors for schools, male and female.

In 1917 the BAI was brought under the auspices of the Education Committee, but continued with its public remit, and by the 1950s was enrolling over 5,000 people per year. Eventually, in 1983, the BAI decamped from John Bright Street to a new sports centre in Highgate, but less than 18 months later finally lost its separate identity. Dolobran AC folded in 1939.

» 1709, and also where the town's earliest known bowling green was located, by the 1730s (where Cherry Street now lies).

Unfortunately no plans or images of any Birmingham cockpits survive. But we do know that the Smallbrook Street pit stayed open until at least 1825, and that on one occasion magistrates ordered the seizure of some 100 people gathered there. They were then roped together and paraded through town as an example.

Returning to cricket – a rural game which evolved into the sport we know today from the early 18th century – the first recorded match in the Birmingham area took place on 15 July 1751. Organised by the 'Society of Cricket Players of Birmingham', it was staged at Holte Bridgman's Apollo Gardens, in the Aston Cross area.

Come the Victorian era, sports such as cricket and bowls would become increasingly gentlemenly. But for working men in the 18th century – and it was only men – cricket and indeed sport of any ilk remained a fairly raucous affair.

Thus in 1776 fifty Birmingham publicans were ordered by magistrates to desist from keeping skittle alleys, billiard tables, tennis courts and roley-poley tables.

Writing in 1783, Birmingham historian William Hutton noted that 'the relaxations of the humbler classes are fives, quoits, skittles and ale', all activities based around taverns and gambling.

19th century sport
In 1801 the population of the town of Birmingham was 71,000. By 1901 – having been incorporated as a city in 1889 and extended its boundaries to Duddeston and Edgbaston in 1838 and Harborne, Balsall Heath, Moseley, Saltley and

Ward End in 1891 – this figure had grown to 522,000.

This included numerous arrivals from all over the British Isles, seeking work in what would become known as the 'city of a thousand trades'. With them they brought a whole new set of cultural influences, of which sport would be one.

Still, the old ways took some time to die out. Even though cockfighting was banned in 1849, in April 1865 the *Birmingham Daily Post* reported the arrest of 38 people, 'among them being Colonels, Captains and County Magistrates' at a cockfight at The Queen's Head, 'better known as "Jemmy Shaw's place"'. Later reports suggest cockfighting persisted at The White Lion in Digbeth until the 1870s.

Clandestine dog fights, which caught on following the ban on bull-baiting in 1835, continued well into the 20th century. Birmingham was also said to have been 'the headquarters of provincial pugilism' (that is, bareknuckle fighting) in the early 19th century, again until the authorities clamped down on this 'sport of high and low life blackguards' by the 1850s.

Another common pleasure frowned upon by respectable townsfolk were traditional wakes.

Originally religious festivals, by 1852 these three or four day fairs – held in Deritend, Ashted, Erdington, Smethwick and Moseley – were, according to *Allen's Guide*, 'only recognised and attended by the lower classes, and persons of bad character and depraved habits.'

William Hutton particularly criticised horse racing through the streets during both the Deritend and Chapel Wakes.

The 1835 edition of Hutton's history also added to his original list of working class indulgences 'cards, dominoes, bagatelle, ball, marble and cricket'.

And yet the French writer and traveller Alexis de Tocqueville painted a quite contrasting view of Brummies. 'These folk', he wrote in 1835, 'never have a minute to themselves. They work as if they must get rich in the evening and die the next day... The town itself has no analogy with other English provincial towns; the whole place is... an immense workshop, a huge forge, a vast shop. One only sees busy people and faces brown with smoke. One hears nothing but the sound of hammers and the whistle of steam escaping from boilers.'

For those without 'a minute to themselves', sport was of little consequence. But as the 'busy people' grew wealthier, and as workers gained more free time following the 1847 Factory Act, the need to provide outlets for sober and wholesome activities grew ever greater.

One such response to this was the 'Rational Recreation' movement, which in Birmingham led to the establishment of the Athenic Institute in 1844, an unsuccessful attempt to interest working class men in 'cricket, quoits and other health inspiring sports'. Others considered the promotion of sport to be far too dangerous, a fear heightened in 1855 when an estimated 11,000 youths went on the rampage in Aston Park on the day of the annual Birmingham Steeplechase, previously staged in outlying areas such as Great Barr and Knowle.

Aston Park was the third public park in the Birmingham area, purchased by the council for £19,000. The other two had been

THE DAILY ARGUS. THE POPULAR PAPER FOR THE MIDLANDS. EVERY EVENING. ONE HALFPENNY. No. 1

The Sports Argus.

BIRMINGHAM, SATURDAY, FEBRUARY 6, 1897.

THE DAILY ARGUS is THE PEOPLES PAPER. EVERY EVENING. ONE HALFPENNY. PRICE ONE HALFPENNY.

donated, by CB Adderley in 1856, and by Lord Calthorpe, in 1857. But still the majority of Brummies, confined in back-to-back houses around the town centre, were woefully short of open space.

Conversely, the council was more proactive in responding to the provisions of the 1846 Baths and Wash-houses Act, opening the city's first baths and public laundries at Kent Street and Woodcock Street in 1851 and 1860 respectively. Indeed Birmingham's programme of constructing baths and wash-houses over the next 90 years would be virtually unmatched in urban Britain, leaving a legacy which remains one of the defining characteristics of the city's historic environment.

The eventual triumph of organised, codified sport in Birmingham during the second half of the 19th century came about thanks to improved transport links, the astute patronage of the city's liberal and Quaker politicians and philanthropists, combined with the organisational powers of a coterie of church leaders, white collar workers and small businessmen.

Sport and recreation, these 'busy people' were able to demonstrate, not only promoted health and sobriety. They were also good for community »

▲ No history of Birmingham sport could be written without recourse to the inestimable **Sports Argus**, whose first edition hit the streets on 6 February 1897. And yet the Argus was by no means the city's first sports paper. The earliest, called *Saturday Night*, appeared in 1882 and covered a wide range of popular topics in addition to sport. This was followed a year later by a Saturday evening edition of the *Birmingham Post and Mail*.

By 1915, 48 British towns and cities had their own Saturday 'specials', printed on a variety of coloured papers. The *Argus* turned pink (as did its counterparts in Coventry, Manchester, Newcastle and Southampton). Sheffield and Bristol's were green, Leicester's was buff.

Today, only a few Pink and Green 'Uns survive, with the *Argus* – now part of the Trinity Mirror group based on Weaman Street – claiming the largest Saturday night circulation of all.

Also invaluable as a resource are the photographs of **Albert Wilkes** (*below left*) and his son, **Albert Wilkes Junior** (*below right*), chroniclers of Midlands sport from c.1907 to 1970. Wilkes Senior (1874–1936) took up the camera whilst a player for Aston Villa and England, before setting up studios in Legge Street, West Bromwich, in 1909. He was also a popular singer on the local music hall circuit, and in 1934 was elected a director at Villa Park.

Several of his images, and those of his son's, appear in this book.

▼ Opened in July 1937 by Gracie Fields – to the strains of Mantovani and his Orchestra – **West Heath Lido**, Alvechurch Road, was one of three open air pools built during the lido boom of the 1930s. The others were at Rowheath (1937–87) and Sansome Road, Shirley, which closed after only three years, in 1939. Its main building, now called Lido House, is used as offices and workshops. West Heath Lido, known as the 'Bath Tub', was also shortlived, closing in 1940. The site is now a housing estate.

Open air pools were no passing fad, however. Earlier ones were at Cannon Hill Park (1873–1939), Small Heath Park (1883–1939) and Brookvale Park (1909–26). Two more were at Malvern Hall, Solihull, from the 1940s to 1982, and Stechford Baths, opened 1961 and now an indoor leisure pool.

Birmingham's last surviving lido was Keeper's Pool, which operated from 1887 to 2002 in Sutton Park.

» and industrial relations, and therefore good for business.

A roll call of clubs established during this period speaks for itself: both the Birmingham Amateur Swimming Club and Edgbaston Archery Society, later to adopt lawn tennis, formed in 1860. They were followed by Moseley FC, the rugby club (1873); Aston Villa (1874); Small Heath Alliance, later Birmingham City (1875); The Priory Tennis Club (1875); Birchfield Harriers (1877); West Bromwich Strollers, later Albion (1879); Warwickshire County Cricket Club (1882) and the Birmingham Anglers Association (1883). Several golf clubs followed during the 1890s, in Moseley, Harborne, Kings Norton, Olton and Sutton Park, plus the Midlands Sailing Club, at Edgbaston Reservoir, in 1894.

The 'best governed city in the world', as Birmingham became known in political circles, was also one of the best organised at a sporting level.

Most famously, it was a Birmingham-based football director – the Scottish draper, William MacGregor of Aston Villa – who was the guiding force behind the foundation of the world's first football league, on 17 April 1888, in Manchester.

Local administrators played similarly key roles at a national level in gymnastics and cycling, while the solidly middle class Birmingham Athletic Club, founded in 1866, was responsible for organising the area's first national sporting event, the Annual Festival of the National Olympian Association, in June 1867. (The NOA's first festival had been staged the previous year in London.) The festival athletics were held at the Aston Lower Grounds, one of several privately owned, multi-purpose sports grounds competing for events in the latter half of the century. The swimming took place at Kent Street Baths, with gymnastics, boxing and fencing staged at the Town Hall.

With influential supporters such as the MP, Sir George Dixon, the Birmingham Athletic Club also lobbied for physical exercise to be entered onto the curriculum of local Board Schools. This was adopted in 1886, after which the form of exercise developed became known nationally as the 'Birmingham Drill.' The city thereafter became a centre for the training of physical education teachers, particularly women, following the foundation of Anstey College, Halesowen in 1897, later moved to King's Norton in 1907. Meanwhile, the city's first club for female cyclists formed in 1901.

At a senior level, the most significant cultural trend of the latter decades of the century was the advent of mass spectator sport.

In Birmingham this had first manifested itself with crowds of up to 30,000 attending horse races at temporary courses in locations such as Olton, Moor Hall Park and Hall Green. Five figure crowds and large numbers of the local betting fraternity also flocked to athletics at the Aston Lower Grounds, the Portland Road Grounds and the Bournbrook Grounds, before, in the 1890s, football finally emerged as the city's favourite sport.

This new mania for regular spectating led, in turn, to the creation of the city's first major purpose-built sports venues: Edgbaston cricket ground in 1886, Bromford Bridge racecourse (1895), Villa Park (1897), The Hawthorns (1900) and St Andrew's (1906). One characteristic shared by these grounds was that each was designed and built in ad hoc fashion, without ostentation. Neither Edgbaston nor Bromford Bridge, in particular, were as sophisticated as their counterparts in London or Manchester.

20th century sport

It is a sobering thought that while several of the Birmingham sportscapes in use today date back to the 19th century – most notably the grass courts of the Edgbaston Archery and Lawn Tennis Society (the oldest in the world) – our researches have identified few surviving sports-related buildings from before 1900, most notably a tennis pavilion at the Edgbaston Priory Club, possibly from the 1880s, and the clubhouse of Sutton Coldfield Golf Club, dated 1897.

This deficit is, however, compensated by the sheer quality of early 20th century buildings extant in the area.

Such examples include the Men's Pavilion (1902) and Girls' Baths (1904) at Bournville; the Moorpool Hall skittles alley (1913); the Billiard Hall, West Bromwich (1913) and the public baths   »

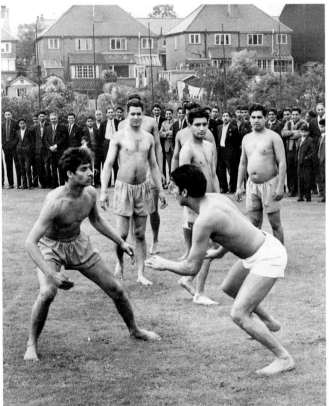

▲ Smethwick's Asian community turns out at **Hadley Fields** for a kabaddi match in July 1965. Similar to British Bulldog, the game consists of two teams of eight players. Attackers try to touch an opponent and return to base while holding their breath and chanting 'Kabaddi Kabaddi' (meaning 'holding breath'). The NIA staged the world's first indoor tournament in 1993, but using the rectangular pitch now favoured by players in India, Pakistan and the Far East.

Immigrants have contributed greatly to Birmingham sport. Scots were prominent in establishing Association football during the 1870s, while German and Jewish Brummies were active in gymnastic circles. More recently, Afro-Caribbeans have been at the forefront of local athletics and football, but less so in cricket than was the case in July 1963 (*below*), when the visit of the West Indies to **Edgbaston** provided the city with an early taste of 'carnival cricket'.

LEWIS'S Seventh Annual 25 miles Outer Circle ROAD WALK SATURDAY JULY 13 1935

▲ Birmingham has a long and honourable tradition of staging sports events on the city's streets. The annual **Outer Circle Road Walk**, sponsored by Lewis's department store from 1929–39, started at The Holte Hotel in Witton Lane, Aston, finishing 25 miles later – via Handsworth, Harborne, Cotteridge, Yardley, Bromford and Erdington – with a single lap of the track at Villa Park in front of crowds gathered for the annual Birmingham charity sports meeting.

In the 1935 event there were 155 entrants from all over the Midlands, including teams from Lozells Harriers, Dunlop and the Magnet Club (GEC).

Today's equivalent is a rather larger affair. Staged on the Whitsun Bank Holiday, in 2005 the BRMB Walkathon attracted an estimated 10,500 entrants.

▲ Redevelopment of Birmingham's inner ring road in the 1970s offered the intriguing possibility of turning the centre into a giant sports arena. The **Birmingham Marathon**, or Brum Run, of September 1981 (*top*) was one of the first events to test this notion. More spectacular, and controversial, was the staging of the first **Halfords Superprix** in August 1986 (*above*), featuring Formula 3 cars on a 2.5 mile course. This was the first time public roads had ever been used for motor racing on the British mainland. But despite crowds of around 60,000, heavy rain marred the race, and there were numerous accidents in subsequent years. The organisers also had to provide local residents with free ear plugs. The last Superprix ran in 1990.

» at Woodcock Street (1902), Moseley Road (1907) and Nechells (1910). Also outstanding from the inter war period are the bowling greens and pavilions at The Black Horse pub, Northfield (1929) and The Maggies, Hall Green (1935), plus Kent Street Baths and Smethwick Baths (both 1933).

To this list might have been added the unique Trinity Road Stand at Villa Park, built 1922–24 (*see opposite*). However, this was demolished in 2000 after attempts to have it listed were turned down.

But sporting heritage need not be measured solely in terms of architectural merit. The actions of individuals, the evolution of trends, and not least the actual impact of specific events can also be woven into the collective sporting conscience.

Concerning the contribution of individuals, as we learn in Chapter Three, between 1880 and the 1930s the Cadbury family's provision of sports and recreational facilities for workers at Bournville, and for the Birmingham public in general – their donation of the Lickey Hills open space in 1904 being just one example – was to have a lasting effect on the sporting character of large parts of the city, and one which still resonates today.

Moreover, the Cadburys' example inspired other major companies in the region to follow suit by creating a chain of works grounds and facilities without equal in Britain.

Several of these grounds were located in areas absorbed into the city's boundaries as a result of the Greater Birmingham Act of 1911, such as Aston, Witton and King's Norton (an expansion which made Birmingham Britain's second largest city, outstripping Glasgow, Manchester and Liverpool).

This was followed by a fresh wave of migration, largely from Scotland, Ireland and Wales, as vast factories on the outskirts – the likes of Austin's at Longbridge and Dunlop's at Erdington – expanded their workforce.

As a result, by the 1950s, a decade of full employment and industrial prosperity, Birmingham could claim phenomenal levels of grassroots sporting activity: for example, the world's largest works football association, and even the world's largest table tennis league (comprised of 300 clubs and 9,000 players). The city's angling association was also the world's largest, with 68,000 members by the 1970s.

And yet it would not last. Once the age of television, car ownership and DIY kicked in, works sport started to decline, until a colossal downturn in the city's manufacturing base during the 1980s caused participation levels to plummet almost in direct proportion to the rise in unemployment.

(An earlier casualty of financial pressure was Bromford Bridge, closed in 1965, thereby leaving the city without a racecourse for the first time since 1740.)

Concurrent with these social shifts came the closure of several of the city's Victorian and Edwardian public baths, to be replaced by multi-purpose 'leisure centres' in the outer suburbs.

Inevitably, fads and fashion have played a part in shaping the city's sporting scene. One example was roller skating; all the rage in the Edwardian era, yet virtually extinct by the 1920s. Speedway, introduced from Australia in the late 1920s, also failed to last the course, being last seen at Perry Barr during the 1980s.

Rather more hardy has been greyhound racing, imported from the USA, also in the 1920s. Birmingham is now the only city outside London to have two tracks, at Hall Green and Perry Barr.

Finally, concerning events, one of the defining aspects of the city's more recent sporting development has been the council's thirst for staging international sport.

Birmingham's private clubs already have a long tradition of staging such events. Since the 1920s three Edgbaston tennis clubs have hosted Davis Cup matches, with the Edgbaston Priory acting as the venue for the annual DFS Classic for women since 1982. Edgbaston's cricket ground staged the first of its many Test Matches in 1902, while Villa Park hosted matches in both the 1966 World Cup and the 1996 European Championships.

But what council leaders appeared to crave most from the 1970s onwards was an arena or stadium befitting the city's international status.

First came plans for an arena at Snow Hill in 1973, then at Perry Barr's new Alexander Stadium, as part of a bid for the 1982 Commonwealth Games. Though unsuccessful, Birmingham did gain its first arena in 1991, with the opening of the National Indoor Arena (*right*), the largest and costliest building of its type in Britain at the time.

Further bids for both the 1992 and 1996 Olympic Games, based around a stadium at Bickenhill, by the National Exhibition Centre, also failed, as did a bid, in 1996, for Bickenhill to become the site of a new national stadium, to replace Wembley. Yet almost like punch drunk boxers not knowing when they were beaten, local »

Dutch supporters pass by Villa Park's Trinity Road Stand during Euro '96. Four years later the stand, designed in the 1920s by Archibald Leitch, would be demolished. Rather less attractive, but certainly more adaptable, is the £51 million NIA (*left*), by the American architects HOK Sport. This has staged events featuring over 25 different sports since opening in 1991. Beneath the main auditorium, which seats from 8,000 to 13,400 depending on the event, is a 1,480 square metre sports hall, used seven days a week by the local community.

›› politicians and strategists picked themselves off the floor and squared up to a fresh set of goals. While Manchester went on to host the 2002 Commonwealth Games in their stunning new, publicly funded City of Manchester Stadium, and London – with £120 million of lottery funding already secured for the rebuilding of Wembley – proceeded to win the right to stage the 2012 Olympics, Birmingham's strategy focused on three main areas.

These were the enhancement of the NIA's already impressive roster of indoor events, particularly athletics and tennis, together with planning for a new flagship stadium, most likely in the Bordesley area (*see below*), possibly in tandem with the provision of a much needed 50 metre indoor swimming pool.

In 2006 the City Council was also contemplating yet another bid for a major international event, the Commonwealth Games.

If such events were awarded for pluck and persistence alone, or indeed for the depth and diversity of the host city's sporting heritage, then Birmingham will surely, one day, achieve its dream.

▲ Watch this space – **Wheels Park**, Saltley, north of St Andrew's (*top left*), is a 38 acre haven for fans of wheeled sports. Opened in 1981 on a contaminated site, its various tracks and pads have been used for go-karting, speedway, BMX, roller hockey and skate boarding. It also has Britain's only purpose built speed skating track.

An unusual example of a late 20th century designed sportscape, the park's location was identified in 2005 as the site for a new casino and stadium. Though the casino has since been ruled out, a new stadium may yet emerge. If so, it is hoped that space will be found for the Wheels Park concept to continue elsewhere, especially in a city where wheels have for so long formed part of the local economy.

1. former **Rolfe Street Baths** Black Country Living Museum (*142*)
2. **The Billiard Hall** St Michael Street (*123*)
3. **The Hawthorns** Birmingham Road (*70-71*)
4. **Handsworth Golf Club** Sunningdale Close (*88*)
5. **Frames 6 Snooker Club** Soho Road (*122*)
6. **Maximum's Snooker Club** Kingstanding Road (*125*)
7. **Alexander Stadium** Walsall Road (*47*)
8. **UCE Pavilion** Moor Lane (*91*)
9. **Perry Barr Greyhound Stadium** Aldridge Road (*42-44,46*)
10. **Villa Park** Trinity Road (*48-51*)
11. **Magnet Centre** Park Approach (*77*)
12. former **Nechells Baths** Nechells Park Road (*142-43*)
13. former **Bromford Bridge paddock** Stratford Walk (*118/121*)
14. **Smethwick Baths** Thimblemill Road (*139*)
15. **Hadley Stadium** Waterloo Road (*72*)
16. **Portland Road Pavilions** Portland Road (*84*)
17. **Edgbaston Reservoir** (*96-97*)
18. **Thomas Fattorini Ltd**. Regent Street (*101*)
19. **Joseph Hudson & Co**. Barr Street (*106*)
20. former **Gothic Works (Vaughton & Sons)** Livery Street (*102*)
21. **Woodcock Street Baths** (*131/133*)
22. former **Kent Street Baths** (*130/131/138*)
23. **St Andrew's** Cattell Road (*68-69*)
24. former **Small Heath Baths** Green Lane (*130/134*)
25. **Harborne Baths** Lordswood Road (*132*)
26. **The Bell Inn Bowling Club** Old Church Lane (*108*)
27. **Munrow Sports Centre** Birmingham University (*26*)
28. **Edgbaston Archery & Lawn Tennis Society** Westbourne Road (*115*)
29. **'Fairlight'** 8 Ampton Road (*114*)
30. **Edgbaston Priory Club** Priory Road (*117*)
31. **KES School Pavilion** Eastern Road (*90*)
32. **Edgbaston County Cricket Ground** Edgbaston Road (*18,22-25*)
33. **Balsall Heath Baths** Moseley Road (*135-37*)
34. **Frames 2 Snooker Club** Walford Road (*124*)
35. **Sparkhill Baths** Stratford Road (*140*)
36. **Moseley Ashfield CC** Yardley Wood Road (*86*)
37. **Moseley Golf Club** Springfield Road (*89*)
38. **Transport Stadium** Wheelers Lane (*85*)
39. **Hall Green Greyhound Stadium** York Road (*74-75*)
40. **The Moorlands** Sherwood Road (*73*)
41. **The Maggies** Shirley Road (*113*)
42. **Robin Hood Golf Club** St Bernard's Road (*89*)
43. **Solihull Bowling Club** The George Hotel, The Square (*110*)
44. **Alan Lee Pavilion** Solihull School (*91*)
45. **Shirley Golf Club** Stratford Road (*90/120*)
46. **Men's Pavilion** Bournville Lane (*34*)
47. **Girls' Baths** Bournville Lane (*36-37*)
48. former **Bournville Lane Baths** (*142*)
49. **Rowheath Pavilion** Heath Road (*38-39*)
50. **Northfield Baths** Bristol Road South (*140*)
51. **The Black Horse** Bristol Road South (*112*)

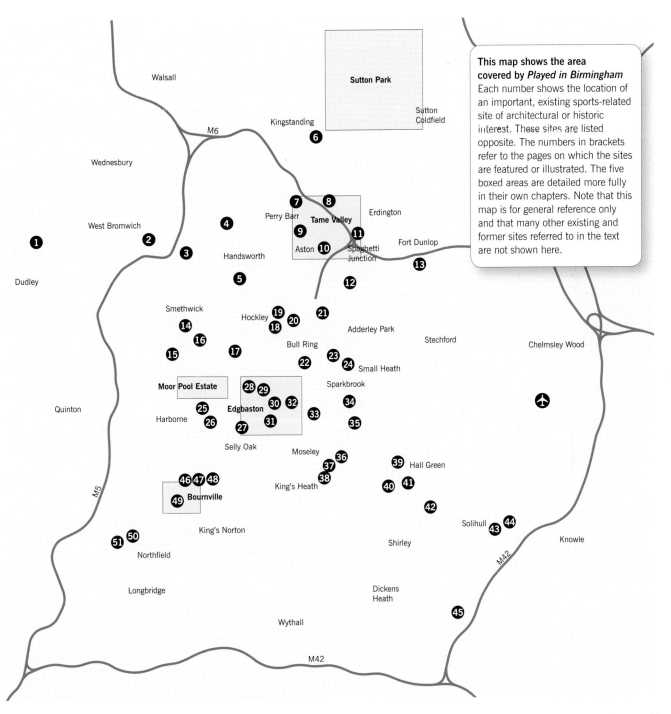

This map shows the area covered by *Played in Birmingham*. Each number shows the location of an important, existing sports-related site of architectural or historic interest. These sites are listed opposite. The numbers in brackets refer to the pages on which the sites are featured or illustrated. The five boxed areas are detailed more fully in their own chapters. Note that this map is for general reference only and that many other existing and former sites referred to in the text are not shown here.

Sutton Park

Walsall

Kingstanding

Sutton Coldfield

6

M6

Wednesbury

7 **8**

Erdington

Perry Barr

Tame Valley

West Bromwich

4

2

9

Fort Dunlop

1

3

Aston **10**

11

Spaghetti Junction

13

Dudley

Handsworth

5

12

Smethwick

19

Hockley

20

21

Adderley Park

Stechford

Chelmsley Wood

14

18

16

Bull Ring

15

17

22

23

24 Small Heath

Sparkbrook

Moor Pool Estate

28 **29**

Quinton

25

30 **32**

34

Edgbaston

33

Harborne

26

31

35

27

Selly Oak

Moseley

36

37

39 Hall Green

38

M5

46 **47** **48**

King's Heath

40 **41**

49 **Bournville**

42

Solihull

44

King's Norton

43

Knowle

51 **50**

Northfield

M42

Longbridge

Shirley

Dickens Heath

45

Wythall

M42

Chapter Two

Edgbaston

Edgbaston County Cricket Ground is Birmingham's oldest international sports venue. During its first Test Match, in May 1902, Australia were bowled out for 36 runs – their lowest ever total – before rain forced a draw. The Thwaite Scoreboard, shown here during England's more recent, scintillating victory over Australia during the epic Ashes series of 2005, is a 1989 replica of the 1938 original.

In sporting circles, even amongst those with no direct knowledge of Birmingham, the name of Edgbaston is renowned.

Edgbaston cricket ground has been staging Test matches since 1902. The first ever games of lawn tennis were played in the garden of an Edgbaston house in or shortly after 1859. The Edgbaston Archery and Lawn Tennis Society claims to be the world's oldest tennis club to be playing on its original grounds. (For the reason, tennis forms its own chapter.)

Other sports played in the area – both at well-appointed private clubs and at facilities belonging to the City Council, Birmingham University, West Midlands Police, plus no fewer than eight public schools – include rugby, football, hockey, athletics, bowls, golf, croquet, fives and swimming.

That so much sporting activity should be concentrated in the area is, in itself, worthy of note.

Rather more remarkable, however, is the fact that, as the aerial view opposite illustrates, Edgbaston's open, recreational spaces are exceptionally close

to the city centre, yet have survived the otherwise rampant urbanisation of the 20th century.

They have done so, by and large, because great swathes of Edgbaston have been, or still are, in the ownership of a single landlord, the Calthorpe Estate.

It is therefore on this estate's borders, hardly more than a mile from the Town Hall, that we begin our survey of Birmingham's sporting heritage, among the elite.

Calthorpe Estate's origins go back to 1717, when a well-travelled merchant, Sir Richard Gough, purchased 1,700 acres of mainly farmland for £20,400. This included Edgbaston Hall, rebuilt by Gough and now the clubhouse of Edgbaston Golf Club.

The first lease to build on the estate followed in 1786, during the lifetime of Gough's grandson, Sir Henry Gough-Calthorpe (who became the first Lord Calthorpe ten years later). But it was only after George, the 3rd Lord Calthorpe (1787–1851) inherited the estate in 1807 that the character of Edgbaston as we know it today started to emerge.

No doubt mindful of how the once exclusive Colmore and Gooch Estates in the town centre were being rented out to businesses and workshops, Lord Calthorpe resolved to create an estate populated only by people of an 'appropriate social class'. Thus agricultural tenants were gradually but deliberately ousted by 'gentlemen and tradesmen'.

With its fast draining soil, fine views across the surrounding countryside and its relative immunity from the noxious fumes of nearby industry (thanks to prevailing winds), Edgbaston was to become a haven for Birmingham's rapidly growing monied classes. No commercial or industrial concerns, nor any housing for the lower orders, were to be permitted within its borders.

Initially development was gradual, until a period of almost continual local prosperity saw Edgbaston's population rise from 6,609 in 1841 to 22,760 in 1881. Steady acquisition of land, meanwhile, expanded estate control to 2,500 acres, or 85 per cent of Edgbaston parish. »

The Calthorpe Estate has long acted as a green buffer to the not-so-distant city centre. To identify the area's sporting locations, compare this view – taken from the southern, Selly Oak side of Birmingham University – with the map on page 21. In the upper centre of the image is Edgbaston Golf Club, closer to the city centre than any other in Britain.

» 'Edgbaston,' declared the first issue of *Edgbastonia* magazine, in 1881, 'is unquestionably the fashionable suburb of Birmingham. The fact that the land is the property of one man, who will permit none but first class houses to be erected, renders it the favourite site for the residencies of independent persons and the wealthier classes of professional men, merchants and traders.'

Within this new Birmingham Belgravia, with its substantial villas, lawns and gardens, a network of refined sports and pastimes soon evolved. In 1825 a bowling green and quoits ground was laid out near the junction of Highfield Road and Harborne Road, 'supported by a select body of subscribers'. In the 1850s, as the Central Edgbaston Bowling Club, the bowlers relocated a short distance to the centre of the street block, where they remain today.

Another mainstay of modern Edgbaston life established during this period was the Botanical Gardens, opened in 1832. It was within their grounds that in 1860 the Edgbaston Archery Society formed. The Society added croquet to its activities in 1870, and the brand new game of lawn tennis three years later (*see Chapter 13*).

Following this, in 1878 the Edgbaston Cricket and Lawn Tennis Club set up on what is now Edgbaston Park Road, followed in the 1880s by the Priory Lawn Tennis Club, on Sir Harry's Road, and by Warwickshire County Cricket Club, who took up residence on the eastern fringe of the Calthorpe Estate in 1886.

Six years later the Birmingham Athletic Club bought 25 acres of land in the Pebble Mill area, and in 1907 the Harborne Polo Club laid out grounds opposite the County Cricket Ground, where they started a tennis section, later to become the Tally Ho! Tennis Club.

With the exception of the County Cricket Ground, where members of the public were admitted, all these sports grounds were reserved for essentially middle class users.

But the Calthorpe Estate was not entirely exclusive in its outlook.

Apart from supporting various voluntary societies and charitable causes, in 1857 the 4th Lord Calthorpe (1790–1868), donated 31 acres of land for the town's second public park, Calthorpe Park (after Adderley Park opened in 1856).

Calthorpe Park's level expanses and accessible location made it particularly popular among exponents of the newly codified Association football. In the 1860s these included players from the Birmingham Clerks Association, who in 1873 formed the area's first club of note, Calthorpe FC.

Because the club was prohibited by the Calthorpe Estate from charging spectators however, by 1876 they had switched their games to yet another newly created venue in the area, the Bournbrook Grounds, behind the Bournbrook Hotel, on Bristol Road, Selly Oak.

With tracks also for cycling and athletics, the Bournbrook Grounds staged the first ever Birmingham and District Challenge Cup Final, in March 1877. Stafford Road from Wolverhampton were beaten 3-2 by Wednesbury Old Athletic, in front of a crowd of 2,500.

Another attraction was Cannon Hill Park, donated to the people of Birmingham in 1873 by a wealthy Edgbaston spinster, Louisa Ryland. In a corner of the park by the River Rea Birmingham's first public outdoor swimming pool was created.

Edgbaston thus evolved as a pleasure ground not only for its residents, but for the people of Birmingham generally.

This influx increased during the 20th century once Edgbaston became home to a formidable collection of schools. King Edward's School, which had owned playing fields at Eastern Road since 1872, relocated from New Street to Bristol Road in 1935. Edgbaston High School for Girls, where some of Birmingham's few remaining grass hockey pitches may be found, opened on its current site in 1962.

Since 1900 the Calthorpe Estate has contracted. Tracts of land have been sold off (for example to Warwickshire CCC in 1919) or donated (to the university in 1900). The ban on commerce has also been eased, as the high-rise office blocks along Hagley Road attest.

There are, as a result, no guarantees that Edgbaston's sports clubs will remain immune from development pressures. The site of the old Tally Ho! Tennis Club, vacated in 1990, has, for example, recently been built over by a mixed office, residential, hotel and leisure scheme.

Even so, what remains of the Calthorpe Estate – a total of 607 hectares – still contains one of Britain's largest urban conservation areas (396 hectares), numerous listed buildings, no fewer than five sites on the Register of Historic Parks and Gardens, and a Nature Reserve designated as a Site of Special Scientific Interest.

No mechanism currently exists whereby any one area can be categorised as one of Special Sporting Interest.

But if there were, Edgbaston would be a prime candidate.

1. **Edgbaston Croquet Club** (1922–)
2. **West House School** (c.1900–)
3. **Edgbaston High School Games Field** (c.1922–)
4. **Edgbaston Archery and Lawn Tennis Society** (1860–)
5. **Hallfield School** (1936–)
6. **8 Ampton Road** (reputed site of world's first lawn tennis match (c.1859) (*see page 114*)
7. **Suburban Cricket Club** (c.1880s–c.1920)
8. **Edgbaston Priory Club** (c.1880s–)
9. **Tally Ho! Bowls Club** (1997–)
10. **Priory School** (1936–)
11. **Edgbaston Golf Club** (1936–)
12. **Edgbaston Cricket and Lawn Tennis Club** (1878–1967)
13. **Munrow Sports Centre** (1966–)
14. **Birmingham University sports ground** (1909–)
15. **Bournbrook Grounds** (c.1870s–c.1900)
16. **King Edward's High School for Girls** (1940–)
17. **King Edward's School fives courts** (c.1935–) and **swimming pool** (1952–)
18. **King Edward's School** (1935–)
19. **King Edward's School Eastern Road sports ground** (1872–) (*see page 90*)
20. **YMCA/Birmingham University Eastern Road sports ground** (c.1914–)
21. **Harborne Polo Club** (1907–1930s) / **West Midlands Police** (c.1930s–) (*see page 82*)
22. **Cannon Hill Open Air Pool** (1873–1939) (*see page 29*)
23. **Tally Ho! Tennis Club** (1907–90)
24. **Edgbaston County Cricket Ground** (1886–)
25. **Edgbaston Indoor Cricket Centre** (2000–)
26. **Raglan Road cricket ground** (c.1880s–c.1900)
27. **Calthorpe Park** (1857–)

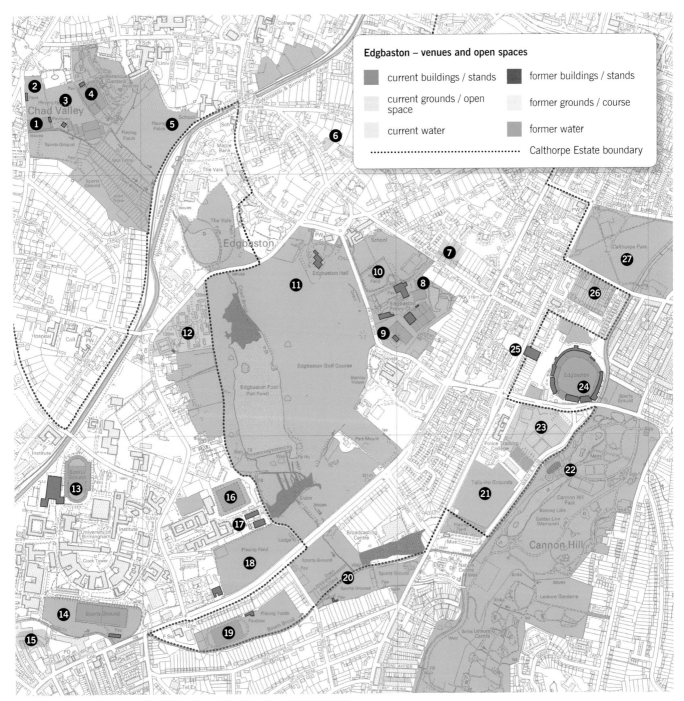

Edgbaston – venues and open spaces

- current buildings / stands
- current grounds / open space
- current water
- former buildings / stands
- former grounds / course
- former water
- .... Calthorpe Estate boundary

Edgbaston County Cricket Ground is nowadays far removed from traditional visions of English cricket, and is certainly quite different from the ground as it appears in these photographs, taken by Albert Wilkes Jnr. during the early 1950s. Shown above is the iron and timber double-decker West Stand, built for the ground's first Test Match, against Australia, in 1902. By the end of what proved to be an unusually wet summer Warwickshire had to make a public appeal for £3,000 to recoup its costs. The stand itself gave sterling service however, until it was finally taken down in 1957.

▼ **Warwickshire County Cricket Club** settled at **Edgbaston** in 1886, three years after the club's formation in Leamington Spa.

Among the founders was a Birmingham schoolteacher, William Ansell. He argued that compared with Leamington, or indeed Warwick, Birmingham offered the new club a greater support base, superior transport links and, crucially, a higher concentration of potential professional players from among the ranks of the Birmingham Association of Cricket Clubs (which Ansell had also been instrumental in establishing).

Various sites in the city were considered, the first being the Aston Lower Grounds (*see page 48*). But after a trial Warwickshire match there in 1882, the wicket was much criticised, as was the ground's proximity to the border with Staffordshire. Attention then turned to the YMCA ground, on Bristol Road, and the Wycliffe Club ground, on Pershore Road.

But it was an offer from Lord Calthorpe of 12 acres of 'rough grazing land' on the banks of the River Rea that won the vote. The terms were attractive – a 21 year lease at £5 per annum – as were the surroundings.

Edgbaston's first game took place in June 1886. A 100 ft long timber stand – seen below to the left – was erected at a cost of £200, next to which was added the pavilion, the core of which is also discernible below, with its clock tower dating from 1888.

Initially only seven of the site's 12 acres were used for cricket, the rest being set aside for tennis, bowls, lacrosse and even baseball. There was also, intriguingly, an attempt to rival other venues in the city, such as the Aston Lower Grounds and the Bournbrook Grounds, by staging football. At that time several leading cricket grounds, including Bramall Lane, Sheffield and Trent Bridge, Nottingham, hosted football clubs in order to capitalise on this fast growing spectator attraction.

But while Edgbaston did stage the Birmingham and District Challenge Cup Final in 1887 (in which Aston Villa beat Wolves) and, in the same competition, the 1891 semi-final (between Villa and WBA), watched by 11,000, the ground's own newly formed club, Warwick County, failed to make an impression, and there would be no more football matches after 1892.

This setback aside, Edgbaston's facilities were steadily expanded. A substantial bank of terracing built up on the east, or River Rea side, in 1889, was joined by a double-decker stand (*seen left*), in 1902

(the same year Ansell finally stood down as Honorary Secretary). At that stage Warwickshire claimed to be able to accommodate 20,000 spectators 'in comfort'.

Further improvements took place after the club bought the ground's freehold from the Calthorpe Estate in 1919, for £5,000 (although the family connection continued when Lord Calthorpe's son, Freddie, was appointed club captain in 1920).

Of particular note was the erection of the Thwaite Scoreboard in 1938 (*shown below*) and the Thwaite Gates on Edgbaston Road, both named after the club's benefactor, Dr Harold Thwaite (later the club president). That same year a bell from the defunct Harborne Somerville Cricket Club was installed atop the pavilion, from where it still chimes today.

By then, however, Edgbaston had fallen behind its counterparts,

particularly Trent Bridge, and had not staged a Test Match since 1929. Nor, despite winning the County Championship in 1951, were Warwickshire able to fund major plans they drew up in 1946 (although they did build up the ground's open terraces using rubble from nearby bomb sites).

The turning point came in 1953, and not without controversy.

Launched by the Supporters' Association, the Warwick Football Pools scheme (based on those already established in football) had originally been rejected by the club's more staid committeemen as 'an undignified method of obtaining funds'. This, it should be noted, was some time before most cricket clubs had considered any type of fundraising.

But Warwickshire's pioneering efforts proved to be a huge success, contributing over £1 million to

ground redevelopments in its first 20 years alone. By the 1970s the scheme was being run by some 7,000 agents, selling to over 300,000 members

Down came the old West Stand in 1957 – the year that Test cricket returned to Edgbaston – to be replaced over the years by an array of new stands, executive suites, dining and conference facilities, together with an indoor cricket school and a colts ground, laid out on land purchased in 1961 from a local school, on the eastern banks of the River Rea.

So it was that Warwickshire cast off its rather conservative reputation and, in the process – echoing the spirit of the city's iconic Rotunda and brave new Bull Ring Shopping Centre – turned Edgbaston into a beacon of thrusting modernity, a very model for progressive thinkers within British sport.

In common with most cricket grounds Edgbaston features numerous memorials, including this statuette of bowler Eric Hollies (a player from 1932–57). Sculpted by Frank Forster, it forms part of the club museum, the only one of its kind in Birmingham sport. (There is also a Hollies Croft – and a Dollery Drive, Wyatt Close and Foster Way – opposite the ground on Pershore Road, overlooked by high rise blocks named Boundary House, Century Tower and Wickets Tower.) Also honoured is the Smethwick-born bowler, Sydney Barnes, whose ashes are encased in the Sydney Barnes Wicket Gate, located at the spot where he first entered the ground in 1894.

▶ Warwickshire's commercial nous may have transformed the **Edgbaston County Cricket Ground** since the 1950s, but in common with most English cricketing venues it remains a hotchpotch of stands – eleven in total – with no coherent style. And yet the ground's credentials are those of a major stadium. It boasts 22,000 seats, 52 executive boxes, two ballrooms, an excellent museum and library, expansive hospitality areas and generous car parks.

But the pavilion remains a poor advert for the club. Largely dating from the 1950s (though the original pitched roof, bell tower and spirelet remain visible, if somewhat overwhelmed, by later adjuncts), it is a building bereft of beauty; inefficient, chaotic and cramped.

From the naming of the stands and gates, and in the discreet memorials around the ground, Edgbaston's real heritage value lies in its longevity and location, not in its architecture. The new Eric Hollies Stand (*opposite*) is a move in the right direction. But Edgbaston still lacks the focus that only a masterful pavilion can provide.

Edgbaston's award winning £2.23 million indoor cricket centre, by Bryant Priest Newman Architects, in association with David Morley Architects (designers of an earlier indoor centre at Lord's Cricket Ground), was completed in 2000. Highly regarded as a training facility for young talent, the extensive use of natural light and ventilation adds to its environmental credentials. It must also be hoped that users, and passers-by, will find at least some inspiration from the somewhat curious artwork on its terracotta-clad west elevation (*right*).

Also by Bryant Priest Newman Architects, in association with engineers Price and Myers, is the £2.1 million Eric Hollies Stand (*left*) – a replacement for the River Rea Stand – another example of cricket's current penchant for 'white and light' architecture. Seating 5,900 spectators on precast terracing, its lightweight aluminium roof – split into four separate modules – features unexpected lateral gaps between the front and rear sections, so that during rain breaks some fans under the canopy still require brollies. That apart, amid the blandness of its neighbours the stand represents a welcome injection of style, which, it is to be hoped, Warwickshire will maintain as the ground develops further.

In common with many parts of the campus the centre is an amalgam of buildings from different periods and by different architects.

The running track dates from 1951. This was joined in 1966 by two sports halls, the work of Chamberlin, Powell and Bon (better known for designing London's Barbican Centre). The first of these is characterised by a distinctive multi-vaulted roof, each vault capped at the southern end by dark red tiled oval panels (*seen here top left*). The second hall (*on the lower left corner of the track*) features a rooftop garden with raised square roof lights and extractors, from where the centre's busy assortment of horizontals, verticals, curves and materials may be enjoyed.

Intriguingly the architects intended to supplement these two buildings with an elevated swimming pool and track side grandstand. Alas these elements were never completed, and all that remains are the proposed pool's supporting pillars, flanking the ramp to the upper levels.

Instead, a rather less ambitious, but still attractive, ground floor pool with prominent water tower was completed in 1976, followed by squash courts in 1978, and a remodelled entrance hall in 1991.

Completing the complex is a single span gymnastics centre (by Henry Boot Design and Build), running parallel with the track and opened in 2001.

Though undoubtedly less stylish than its more innovative neighbours, it is at least free from the design issues that afflict the original 1960s elements of the Munrow Sports Centre, where spectators, competitors and the centre's management alike face a constant battle with leaks and ongoing maintenance problems.

Juxtaposed against the backdrop of Webb and Bell's familiar red brick campanile (and the brutalism of Philip Dowson and Arup Associates' Muirhead Tower, not in view), the Munrow Sports Centre, with the shell-like roof lights of its fitness suite, and its assortment of angles and styles, creates one of the most visually rewarding settings for sport in Birmingham.

▲ Few red brick universities have outdoor sports facilities within their main campus area. **Birmingham University** – first laid out on a 25 acre site donated by Lord Calthorpe in 1900 – has two such areas, both quite admirable.

The first, in front of the Great Hall on Bristol Road, consists of three all-weather surfaces and a rugby pitch which acted as a temporary base for Moseley RFC from 2000–05 (*see page 72*).

The second is situated more discreetly on low-lying ground, in the north of the campus, bordered by Pritchatts Road and the Worcester and Birmingham Canal.

It is on this site that we find Birmingham's most interesting post-war sports complex, the **Munrow Sports Centre**, just one element of a major expansion plan drawn up for the university from 1957 onwards by the architects Sir Hugh Casson and Neville Conder.

◀ There may only be a select few in attendance, but this is a scene from the World Croquet Championships, whose early rounds were staged for the first time at the **Edgbaston Croquet Club** on **Richmond Hill Road**, in August 2005.

With their suburban villas and manicured gardens, Edgbaston and Moseley offered fertile ground for croquet when it took root in Britain in the 1850s (having evolved earlier in France and Ireland).

But croquet lawns also proved ideal for the newly invented sport of lawn tennis, when that too was embraced by the middle classes from the 1870s onwards. Croquet has thus had to be content with minority status ever since.

Now the city's sole surviving club, the Edgbaston Croquet Club is thought to have first played in the grounds of the Plough and Harrow pub, Hagley Road, in 1905.

Among its early members were priests from the adjoining Oratory (where there had also once been a croquet lawn). The club moved to its present site in 1922.

Run entirely by volunteers, there are three full size lawns and a minimalist steel cabin, which replaced a timber pavilion in 1983. But unassuming though its grounds may be, the club enjoys cordial relations with its landlord. Indeed one Lord Calthorpe apparently decreed that there should always be a place where croquet might be played on the estate.

Not that it is any longer the preserve of the idle rich. Modern Association Croquet is highly challenging, said to be a blend of bowls, snooker and chess. (Golf Croquet, a less cerebral variation, is played at the Old Silhillians Club in Warwick Road.) It is also one of the few games where men and women compete on equal terms.

◀ Golf courses are sometimes criticised for their impact upon historic landscapes. But **Edgbaston Park**, home of **Edgbaston Golf Club** since 1936, may be regarded both as an historic landscape, and as an historic sportscape.

The park was first laid out in the 1770s by Sir Henry Gough to designs that were inspired, if not actually drawn up by Capability Brown. Within the park is the Great Pool, thought to have been created in the 16th century, and **Edgbaston Hall**, rebuilt in 1717 by Sir Richard Gough and now Grade II listed. Edgbaston Park is itself listed Grade II on the Register of Historic Parks and Gardens, while the Great Pool is designated a Site of Scientific Interest.

There is also a local nature conservation area on the south and western sides of the pool.

But there is more, because when the golf club moved to the park in 1936 – setting up their clubhouse in Edgbaston Hall (*just visible in the upper centre of the photograph*) – to design their new course they hired Harry S Colt, widely regarded as the Capability Brown of golf course architecture.

Colt, who had already designed such noted courses as Sunningdale, Wentworth, Royal Liverpool and the Eden course at St Andrews, was particularly adept at using existing landscapes to their best advantage, while preserving the natural beauty and character of the site.

At Edgbaston the result is a beautiful, but also challenging course which is, in itself, worthy of preservation as one of the finest examples of Colt's work.

And all this less than two miles from the city centre.

▶ One of Edgbaston's more unusual sporting structures is a block of six **Eton Fives courts**, located within the grounds of **King Edward's School**, on Bristol Road.

Fives – which resembles squash, but played with gloved hands rather than racquets, and by two players in each team – is one of many forms of handball played around the world, its origins in Britain going back to at least the 15th century. Eton Fives, as its name suggests, is a variant derived from Eton College, where generations of boys played the game against the buttressed walls of the chapel.

Eton's first purpose-built courts were constructed in 1840. These at King Edward's date back to the late 1930s. (Currently around 40 schools play the game, which has two other variants, Rugby Fives and Winchester Fives.)

As shown here, each court is divided into two levels by a low step, with ledges on all three walls and a buttress on the left, sometimes called the 'pepper pot'.

The six courts are named after former Chief Masters, among them James Prince Lee, who had earlier taught at Rugby under the noted educational reformer, Thomas Arnold. It was thanks to Prince Lee that the King Edward's governors purchased the school's first playing fields, on Monument Road, Edgbaston, in 1842.

▲ After surveying the private sports grounds of Edgbaston – with further sites still to be detailed in later sections on tennis, bowls and Edgbaston Reservoir – we finish this chapter with one of the area's long forgotten public amenities, the open air pool at **Cannon Hill Park**.

Outdoor pools, the precursors of 1930s lidos, were surprisingly common in the late Victorian period, and in Birmingham, Cannon Hill's was the earliest.

Oval in plan and measuring 216 x 100 ft, it opened in 1873, as did the park – designed by John Gibson, who had trained under Joseph Paxton at Chatsworth – and remained in use until 1939 (by which time there were four other public outdoor pools in the city, none of which survive).

Cannon Hill Park today retains its facilities for tennis, bowls, boating, fishing and indeed a charming, early 20th century octagonal pay booth for 'crazy golf' (*see page 92*).

But the only slight echo of the swimming pool is the central court of the Midlands Arts Centre, built on the site in the mid 1960s and following part of the elliptical plan of the pool as seen here.

Chapter Three

Bournville

George Cadbury, his biographer wrote, 'loved games for themselves but he loved them still more as a physical training necessary to keep one fit for the real business of life'. Thus Cadbury would rise at five to play hockey or football or go swimming or skating for two hours before starting his day's work. This colossal energy, and not least his gifting of vast tracts of open space to the city, played a huge part in shaping the character and geography of Birmingham today.

Bournville in 1897, shortly after the laying out of the Men's and Girls' Recreation Grounds. Running through the site, the Bourn Brook provided the works with plentiful water and fed a pool, which a year later was turned into an outdoor swimming pool. Plots to the north and west have been marked out for housing.

Britain's sporting heritage manifests itself in diverse forms: in architecture, landscape, artefacts and art. But it may also be discerned within the realm of ideas, as an expression of political or moral philosophies, of social and economic strategems.

More often than not, sports historians have to identify these strands from a scattering of evidence. But not so in the Birmingham district of Bournville, the fiefdom of Cadbury's, makers of chocolate, now known as the multinational conglomerate, Cadbury Trebor Bassett.

Even amid the unrelenting flow of modern traffic, the comings and goings of visitors to the Cadbury World themed experience, and the visual clutter of late 20th century industrial and office buildings, the essential homogeneity of Bournville's 'factory in a garden' and its surrounding village, stands out with a rare clarity.

Here is a cornucopia of architectural delights, almost self-contained and surprisingly intact, where one may walk, observe and gain a deep sense of how sport,

recreation and green space were central to the Cadbury family's wider social mission.

Theirs was hardly a unique vision. Several philanthropic businessmen of the 19th century were driven by broadly similar creeds of Christian paternalism allied to capitalistic enterprise in order to provide better working conditions, decent housing and educational opportunities. But it was only in the latter part of the Victorian era that companies began to provide also for their workers' physical recreation.

Titus Salt, for one, provided swimming baths and a gymnasium at his model community of Saltaire in the 1860s. The Great Western Railway similarly built its Swindon

employees a swimming pool in 1869, while in 1885 the London & North Western Railway Company laid out a cycling and athletics track at its Wolverton Works.

Those, and the provisions of other companies, including the Rowntrees in York and William Lever at Port Sunlight in Birkenhead, would soon however be eclipsed by the efforts of the Cadbury brothers, Richard (1836–99) and George (1838–1922).

As is well documented, the Cadbury story began in 1824, when Richard and George's father, John Cadbury, began selling tea, coffee and drinking chocolate in Bull Street. By the 1870s the business had prospered sufficiently to require larger premises.

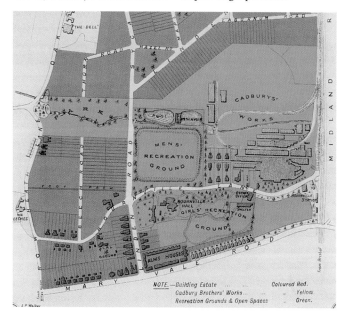

Key to the Cadburys' needs was a pollution free environment, away both from the grime and distractions of the town centre. In common with several other leading Birmingham figures of the time, the Cadburys were ardent Quakers and supporters of the Temperance movement. George even renounced tea and coffee.

Just as significantly, both brothers were passionate about sport and outdoor activity. As early as the 1860s they formed a cricket team, and would happily close their Bridge Street works in order to stage a staff match. They encouraged boys to learn to ride the company's boneshaker, and in 1874, being great walkers themselves, initiated an annual Spring Walk.

So it was that in 1878 the brothers purchased 14.5 acres of farmland beside Bournbrook Hall, three miles south west of the town, alongside the railway and canal leading to Bristol (from whose docks the cocoa was transported).

In a masterstroke of what would today be termed branding, the Cadburys chose to call their new estate 'Bournville' – Bourn after the brook which ran through the site, and 'ville' because French chocolate was then highly prized.

Production at the new factory began in 1879, with sport being organised amongst the 200 or so workers under the auspices of the Bournville Cricket and Football Club, formed in 1883.

Female staff, meanwhile, were allocated their own garden-cum-playground, but were equally encouraged to undertake physical exercise (as was increasingly the norm in wider Birmingham gymnastic circles, years before such gender equality became accepted practice elsewhere).

BOURNVILLE WORKS, 1931.

Even so, facilities were still basic, serving mainly the needs of workers during break times.

By the 1890s Cadbury's had grown into a hugely successful operation, employing nearly 2,000 staff. So that more of them could live close at hand, in 1893 Cadbury's purchased 120 acres of adjacent land for the construction of Bournville Village.

Although designed by the company's newly appointed architect, WA Harvey, the village was financed separately as a model residential development in its own right and was managed after 1900 by the independent Bournville Village Trust. Unlike other factory villages of the period, Bournville was no mere company enclave. In order to ensure a social mix, at least 40 per cent of tenancies were offered to non-Cadbury employees. All tenants, however, were handed a booklet entitled 'Rules of Health', which included a recommendation to walk or exercise in the open air for at least half an hour per day.

As Bournville Village emerged, so too, from 1895–1906, were the estate's recreational areas expanded and enhanced to a level that would be unrivalled by any other British company, and would certainly have been the envy of most public schools.

Exact figures for the company's outgoings on sport and recreation during this period have never been stated explicitly. But it has been reported that by 1905 – the year Cadbury's launched their trademark Dairy Milk chocolate – a staggering 30 per cent of expenditure was committed to activities other than production. »

Bournville's 'Factory in a Garden' depicted in 1931. Despite the factory's expansion since the map of 1897 (*see left*) and the completion of Bournville Village Trust housing to the north, the estate's green spaces had at that stage been preserved. But further expansion since the 1950s has left intact only the Men's Recreation Ground (*shown here as football pitches*) and sections of the Girls' Recreation Ground (*left foreground*). Otherwise, the green areas seen in the right foreground have since been built over or turned into car parks, while housing occupies much of the land east of the canal. That said, Bournville's garden village remains one of the great urban wonders of modern Britain.

▲ Bournville's facilities mirrored the tastes of the Cadbury brothers. George in particular adored cricket and often joined in with staff matches. Hence boys at the factory – who started work at the age of 13 – were allocated equipment and their own field for dinner breaks, as recorded in 1887 (*top*), only eight years after the factory opened.

As a true Victorian gentleman George was also a great advocate of cold baths and outdoor swimming. Hence in 1898 one of the two pools fed by the Bourn Brook and used for cooling in the production process, was converted into a 100 foot long men's swimming pool. Shown above in 1905, with the Men's Pavilion in the distance, it was open from 1–2pm and 5–6pm.

All employees, male and female, were taught how to swim, although from 1905 females had the benefit of a heated indoor pool, to which, not surprisingly, the men soon sought access.

Despite this, the outdoor pool remained in use until 1936, and its basic form can still be seen today.

≫ At the same time, we can only guess at the potential income sacrificed as a result of Cadbury's policy of buying extra land for recreation rather than for housing.

In 1895, for example, the company purchased Bournbrook Hall in order to lay out a 12 acre recreation ground for female staff.

The following year, work began on levelling and laying out the Men's Recreation Ground, thereby providing a further 14 acres for cricket, football and hockey. Two Aston Villa officials, George Ramsay and Fred Rinder, then in the midst of developing their own new ground at Villa Park, were invited to inspect, and were sufficiently impressed to send a team to play the inaugural match on the Bournville ground, in October 1897 (this only months after Villa had won the Double).

The Bournville team that day was itself a new creation. A year earlier the Cadburys had encouraged the formation of a new organisation, the Bournville Athletic Club, to oversee all male sport at the works.

This was followed in 1899 by the Bournville Girls' Athletic and Social Club, and in 1900 by a Youth Club. (Employee numbers at this stage had risen to around 2,700.)

Thus, by the turn of the century, with George Cadbury now chairman following Richard's death in 1899, the stage was set for the construction of the buildings detailed on these pages; that is the Men's Pavilion (1902), the Girls' Baths (1904-5), the Rowheath Pavilion (1924) and Lido (1937), and sundry other sports buildings dotted around the ever expanding Cadbury empire.

George Cadbury never made any pretense that his espousal of sport was solely philanthropic.

As conceded in a biography published in 1923, a year after his death, 'Behind the athletics, the dentistry, the swimming baths, the doctoring, the arrangements for meals, lies a supreme commercial objective – speed of hand coupled with accuracy of eye. These are the qualities which in the workers make the business pay.'

George's son, Edward, clearly agreed. In his seminal 1912 paper 'Experiments In Industrial Organisation' he stated that employees 'should have the desire and opportunities for hobbies and recreation outside their work'.

Physical exercise for employees under the age of 18 was already compulsory within company time. Now all workers were to be encouraged to 'play the game' after hours too.

Which they did, whether willingly or not, in great numbers.

In 1920 an inter-departmental games league commenced. Motor cycle rallies were held in Bournville Lane. There were separate social clubs for clerks and foremen (where billiards and cards were favoured), an Angling Society with 200 members, a camera club and several choral and musical groups. Meanwhile, continuing the tradition begun in 1874, the whole company closed down for a day for the annual Spring Walk to the Lickey Hills.

This almost relentless pursuit of recreation showed no sign of abating after the First World War. Squash courts were opened on Linden Road and a four storey Dining Block completed in 1922. Despite its title, the Dining Block performed a dual role, housing a gymnasium, snooker rooms, a youth club, chess club, a concert hall with 1,050 seats and extensive dressing rooms for girls linked by a subway (still visible, though long closed) under Bournville Lane, leading to the Girls' Recreation Ground. There was even a playground and a block of fives courts on the Dining Block roof.

Yet still this was not enough, for in 1919, as detailed on page 38, work also began on the conversion into playing fields of a further 75 acres at nearby Row Heath Farm.

By the time the new facilities opened in 1924 – two years after George's death, and at a time of growing industrial unrest elsewhere in Britain – sport at Bournville seemed to rank almost as highly as chocolate. Combined membership of the company's adult athletic clubs, for example, totalled over 3,700, at a time when the total workforce numbered around 7,500.

Moreover, the company and the Bournville Village Trust boasted an inventory of no fewer than 17 football pitches, 16 cricket pitches, two rugby pitches, seven hockey pitches, 41 tennis courts, four bowling greens, four netball pitches, two athletic tracks, two croquet lawns, two swimming pools, a fishing pool and a model yacht lake. There were small towns in Britain with less.

And still Bournville grew.

By 1931 it covered 1,455 acres (including 110 acres of recreation grounds) with 2,000 houses and a population of 7,500. Later expansion, mainly in Northfield, Weoley Castle and Shenley Fields, would, by 1955, raise the number of properties to over 3,500, and the Bournville Village Trust to a population of 10,500.

Yet despite this growth, the days when thousands would throng to Bournville's extensive playing fields each week have passed, for reasons well rehearsed in other

quarters: increased car ownership, the advent of television and so on.

But another factor has been the drop in staff numbers. Having peaked at 10,000 in 1938, largely as the result of greater automation it now stands at just 2,500.

This decline has had predictable consequences. In the early 1980s 65 acres at Rowheath were sold for housing and the Rowheath Pavilion only saved after a hard fought campaign by local residents. Another casualty of ths period was Rowheath's lido, closed in 1987.

Meanwhile the old Dining Block, along with its extensive recreational resources, is no more, and the Girls' Recreation Ground, though still essentially intact, has few sporting facilities and is now bordered by office blocks and car parks. The Girls' Baths, though

refurbished externally in 2005, closed in 1982.

Yet although Cadbury's sporting facilities, and to a lesser extent those within Bournville Village, have contracted, it must be emphasised that they remain substantial compared to those of other company sports grounds (as we shall learn in Chapter Eight).

Perhaps instead the greater loss is something rather more intangible. That sense of community which comes from being part of something so immense, so all embracing, so unique as that which the Cadbury dynasty created at Bournville.

'Birmingham's very own chocolate paradise' reads the description offered to visitors to the Cadbury World experience.

To which might once have been added, 'a sporting paradise' too.

'Swedish drill' – as was all the rage in gymnastic circles – outside the Girls' Gymnasium (now the site of the Cadbury Club) in 1902. Like the boys at Bournville, until they turned 18 all girls had to undergo two half hour classes in physical education every week, albeit within company time. Note the rusticated timber decoration on the gymnasium wall, a common Bournville architectural touch.

▶ Resplendent in its chocolate brown and white half-timbered detailing, the **Men's Pavilion** on Bournville Lane, listed Grade II, is probably Britain's finest and least altered Edwardian pavilion.

Built at a cost of £4,000 and opened on 10 June 1902, it was originally named the Coronation Pavilion and was designed by Henry Bedford Tylor, Cadbury's architect from 1904–11. (Among Tylor's other works are the shops and bank on the Green, where the Friends' Meeting House, by Tylor's predecessor, WA Harvey, has an identical octagonal roof turret.)

Despite its almost Alpine grandeur, internally the pavilion appears spartan. The top floor serves primarily as a gymnasium (*see opposite*), though indoor bowls, skittles and badminton are also played there. Extensive use of timber and a copper war memorial impress nevertheless.

In the corner of the ground, a 1933 bronze of Terpischore, by William Bloye, forms the centrepiece of an ornate fountain. Adjacent to this is banked terracing, from where spectators may enjoy proceedings accompanied by the ever present aroma of chocolate.

Truly, this is a palatial sports ground that delights all the senses and one that it is almost impossible to imagine being commissioned in today's economic climate.

Outdoor gymnasiums or 'trim trails' were created in several Birmingham parks and recreation grounds during the 1980s, in the hope of encouraging more members of the public to take exercise. The parallel bars at Bournville (*left*) and their accompanying instructions (*above*) – seemingly carved into ancient stone – are on the Men's Recreation Ground on the corner of Bournville Lane and Linden Road. Rather more high tech, though equally sculptural, fitness trails have recently been installed at Jobs Close Park, Knowle and at Elmdon Park, Solihull. Not for the self-conscious perhaps, but an alternative for those unable to afford gym membership fees.

▲ Compulsory gymnastics for all boys under 18 – as shown in the **Men's Pavilion** in 1905 (*top*) – was geared not only towards fitness but towards teaching how to lift weights and improve co-ordination.

Ball games such as croquet, netball and lawn tennis were also taught, to improve hand and eye co-ordination for women working on the production line. The tennis court shown above c.1905 no longer exists, but both the loggia and pavilion can still be seen in the **Girls' Recreation Ground**, along with the original lily pond.

Apart from being photographed for the monthly *Bournville Works Magazine*, Cadbury workers have long been accustomed to visitors passing through the factory on guided tours. But not all were there simply as chocolate lovers.

In its early years the Men's Recreation Ground staged several well-attended international hockey matches and in summer played occasional host to Worcestershire CCC's First XI (Bournville being just inside the county's former borders). Indeed the pitch was held by many to be the finest in the county.

Large crowds also attended the company's annual Sports Day, established in 1905, and annual Bournville Village Fete, which always culminated in a spectacular fireworks display.

Other visitors, businessmen and politicians came simply to look and learn. One German later wrote to George Cadbury, 'I repeatedly exhibited the pictures you gave me, and was asked... to what the gymnasium, swimming baths, park belonged... and it did not occur to anyone that these places were for the use of factory hands.'

▲ Even in a city noted for its wealth of historic municipal swimming pools, the **Girls' Baths** at Bournville is of exceptional quality. Externally the Grade II listed building has been likened to a Nonconformist chapel, with its cod buttresses and projecting clock tower. Internally, it is flooded with light from the roof and upper storey.

Designed by the company architect GH Lewin and engineered by a fellow employee, Louis Barrow, the baths opened in 1904 and offered, at the time, the largest covered pool in Birmingham, measuring 80 x 46 feet and with a capacity of 105,000 gallons.

There were also 22 'spray baths' (or showers), two slipper baths, 84 changing rooms and hairdryers on both the ground floor and balcony.

Equally impressive was the baths' advanced filtration system, which the engineer had seen fitted at various baths in Manchester and Bury, and its boilers, which heated up the water – sourced from Bourn Brook – to 74° in summer and 76° in winter. Little wonder therefore that, although built for female staff, the men and boys, otherwise confined to the unheated outdoor pool, soon demanded entry.

Within a year they succeeded, but only before 8am on weekdays and between 4–9pm on Fridays. (Mixed bathing, in a company where even the dining rooms were segregated, would be a much later concession.)

In 2006 the baths' future use was in some doubt.

Although the exterior – including the ornate carved panel by Benjamin Creswick (*left*), and a datestone from one of the original cottages built on the site in 1879 – has recently been extensively refurbished, the interior (*see right*) has, alas, lain unused since 1982.

One possible option being considered is to convert it into a health and fitness suite.

◀ Young swimmers pose at the **Girls' Bath** in 1911. That the company built the baths at all was significant.

Until the 1920s most local authorities provided female swimmers with facilities inferior to those of men, while few companies showed interest in women's recreation at all.

Yet by the time the Girls' Baths opened in 1904 female staff at Bournville outnumbered their male colleagues by three to one, and Cadbury's insisted that every one of them not only learnt to swim but also undertook life-saving drill.

(All female employees were also allowed to take one bath per week in company time.)

One consequence of this far sighted policy was that Bournville workers were well placed to teach swimming at other local pools, for example through the firm's association with the pioneering Anstey College of Physical Education, founded for women in 1897, in Halesowen.

Thus Cadbury's policies reaped benefits and helped change attitudes far beyond the confines of Bournville.

Today the interior of the Girls' Baths is a forlorn sight (*left*), as is the similarly disused Stirchley Baths, built further down Bournville Lane on land donated by George Cadbury in 1911 (*see page 142*).

▲ For most companies the sports facilities provided at Bournville would have been deemed sufficient. But in 1919, with Cadbury's workforce approaching 7,500, the Bournville Village Trust began development of a further 75 acres at Row Heath Farm, west of the factory.

At the time of its opening in July 1924 **Rowheath** (*viewed here in 2005 from the south*), boasted an inventory of 14 pitches for football, 13 cricket, four hockey and two rugby, plus 31 tennis courts, two bowling greens, two croquet lawns, an athletics track, a green for clock golf and a boating and fishing lake.

To service this substantial park and sports ground a splendid 145 foot long Italianate pavilion (*opposite*) was built on the highest

point of the ridge along which Heath Road runs.

Statistics show why every one of Rowheath's 450 dressing room coat pegs was needed.

In 1931 the grounds were home to 38 teams for rugby, 38 football, 35 tennis, 32 cricket, 28 bowls, 28 hockey and 25 netball, plus clubs for cross country, swimming and water polo.

On a typical Saturday there could be up to 100 teams and 1,000 players on the site, while on summer weekends the sporting crowds were joined by local residents and Bournville staff enjoying musical performances by various Cadbury's bands playing on the park's two bandstands.

Added to Rowheath's attractions was a modernist lido, completed in

1937 (*see page 40*), south west of the pond.

Since those heady days a decline in usage has required a series of campaigns to save the pavilion.

Sixty five acres, including nine tennis courts, were sold for housing in the early 1980s, including the area now called Long Wood (*seen to the left of the bowling greens, above*). Further housing followed on the lido site after its closure c.1987, facing onto what is now Oak Farm Road (*just below the pond in the centre foreground*).

Various local groups have since then endeavoured to ensure that the pavilion and the pitches are maintained in good order.

As of 2006 that onerous but honourable task rests with the Trinity Christian Centre Trust.

◀ Worthy indeed of its place in the Garden Village is the splendidly trim pavilion of the **Rowheath Bowls Club**. Opened in May 1931, it originally featured a thatched roof (replaced, probably wisely given its exposed location, by the current slates in the 1960s).

As explained in Chapter Twelve, Birmingham is the only place in Britain where both flat and crown greens exist alongside each other within the same site: at the Tally Ho! Club, Edgbaston (*see page 111*) and at the West Midlands Police grounds on Pershore Road (*page 82*). Until 1986 Rowheath shared that unusual distinction, having two flat greens and a crown green served by the same pavilion.

Thereafter only one flat green was maintained, until in 2006 the other, dormant flat green was restored to use owing, happily, to increased demand.

But then Bournville is no ordinary district. While elsewhere in Britain the number of bowling greens is in general decline, in this corner of Birmingham the sport appears to be thriving.

There is a single crown green on the Men's Recreation Ground in Linden Road – its small, chocolate brown, half timbered pavilion echoing its rather grander neighbour, the Men's Pavilion, across the turf – while on the western side of Linden Road two further crown greens are to be found in Bournville Park, itself bequeathed to Birmingham by George Cadbury in 1907.

On the Girls' Recreation Ground, meanwhile, are two flat greens used by Bournville Bowls Club, both laid out in 1986 on former tennis courts.

Another club to have ousted tennis in favour of bowls is at Woodlands Park, west of Rowheath, in the secluded surrounds of Northfield Road, on Bournville's south western edge, where in 2000 a second crown green was laid on a former court.

▲ One of Cadbury's least well documented, and yet architecturally most arresting facilities was **Bournville Lido**. Located to the immediate south of Rowheath lake and opened in 1937 at the peak of Britain's lido building boom – a period documented in a previous title in this series, *Liquid Assets (see Links)* – the open air pool is the only major example of modern 20th century recreational architecture constructed by the company. And yet it was to close after just 50 years and in 1997 was replaced by housing on Oak Farm Road and Lake View Close.

Designed by Edwin Stanley Hall (who also worked on Liberty's of London and at the Ashmoleum Museum, Oxford), the pool measured a modest 100 x 50 feet, with a small children's pool, single storey café and entrance block at the north end. In its heyday the lido staged galas, water polo and national swimming trials.

In the late 1930s Birmingham had no fewer than five open air pools, including West Heath Lido, also opened in 1937, only a mile from Rowheath. Yet by 1945 only two survived, Bournville and Sutton Park. Now, sadly, there are none.

Looking back at the concrete angularity of Bournville Lido – such a contrast to the half-timbered and stuccoed pavilions so characteristic of the rest of the Bournville estate – it is regrettable that compared with other cities, so few examples of 1930s sporting architecture survive in Birmingham.

Yet in other respects the legacy of George Cadbury and his family far outweighs such regrets.

Aside from the still obvious pleasures of Bournville and Rowheath, during the early 20th century the Cadbury family gifted to Birmingham tracts of land so

vast that they significantly shaped both the character and geography of the city as we know it today. These included Bournville Park, in 1907, The Rose and Crown Estate near Rubery, in 1919, and not least, 840 acres of the Lickey Hills, donated to the city in 1904, together with nearby Beacon Hill three years later. Hardly a south Birmingham resident has not, at one time or another, felt the benefit of these high and wild open spaces on the city's edge.

Back towards town, meanwhile, on Bristol Road, Northfield, is **Manor Farm Park**, another public park that once belonged to the Cadburys, formerly the grounds of George and his wife Elsie's family home, Manor House, from 1894 until his death in 1922.

Near the park entrance stands a building instantly recognisable as one from the Bournville architects' office. Adorned with the company's trademark rusticated timber detailing, **The Barn** (*above right*) was used by the Cadburys to host their legendary summer parties.

Up to 25,000 people a year – employees, their families and children from poor homes – were said to have attended these epic jamborees. Up to 700 could be seated in The Barn alone. Children were invited to swim in the fish pond, 50 at a time – girls before tea, boys after. Famously it was written of George's attitude to party-giving at The Barn, 'There could never be too many and they could never be too noisy.'

Today The Barn serves as a storeroom. But in its romantic timbers and its evocation of a tumultuous period in Birmingham's growth, it is a reminder that for all the city's debt to metal-bashing and motor cars, milk chocolate has made its contribution too.

Chapter Four

Tame Valley

Against the odds – Birmingham is Britain's only provincial city to support two greyhound tracks. One is at Hall Green (*see page 75*), the other at Perry Barr (*above*), on the site of what had been, until 1978, the preserve of two legged runners, in the guise of Birchfield Harriers. Confusingly, Harriers' new Alexander Stadium bears the same name as their old one, while there was also, until 1984, an earlier Perry Barr dog track across the road from the present one.

Clusters of sports venues form for a variety of reasons. The influence of the Calthorpe Estate was clearly key to the concentration of middle class, private clubs in Edgbaston. The Cadbury company equally shaped the sporting map of Bournville.

North of the city, three main factors led to the formation of a quite distinctive cluster of venues linked geographically by the winding path of the River Tame.

Firstly, the river itself – whose source is in Rowley Regis and which flows eastwards through Perry Barr to Castle Bromwich, and thereafter up towards Burton-on-Trent – was a vital resource for the area's burgeoning industries from the early 18th century onwards. Iron forges in the Black Country, the colliery in Hamstead and manufacturing in Witton all sourced water from the Tame, and dumped their waste in it.

Small wonder that it was too polluted to support life from as early as the 1860s.

Industrial development inevitably led to a significant rise in the population throughout

the 19th century. Yet much of the river valley remained unsuited to residential development owing to its potential for flooding. Such areas – the Perry Hall Playing Fields for example, formerly the

grounds of the 16th century Perry Hall – were therefore best suited to recreational use.

A second factor was the break up, in 1818, of Aston Park, the former Holte family estate

The LMS Railway's poster for the opening night of the first Perry Barr Greyhound Stadium, in 1928. 'Electric hare coursing' was then in its infancy, perhaps explaining why the link with rural Goodwood was necessary. Two years later Perry Barr also became the location of the first Odeon cinema, opened by Birmingham entrepreneur Oscar Deutsch on Birchfield Road.

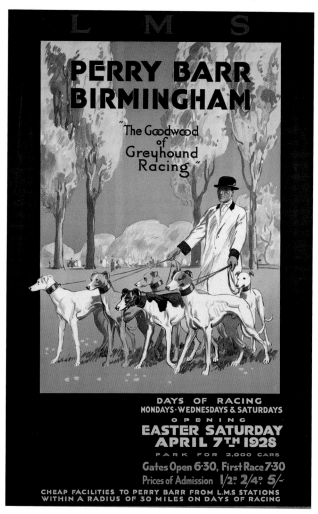

attached to the Jacobean Aston Hall (built by Sir Thomas Holte between 1618–35).

Aston Park's upper grounds were opened to the public in 1858, while the lower grounds, bounded on the east by the Tame, were transformed during the 1860s into the most sophisticated amusement gardens and sports grounds yet seen in the Midlands. The park, lower grounds and a string of grounds in the immediate vicinity nurtured at least eight of the area's earliest football clubs in the 1870s, one of whom, Aston Villa, would become England's leading club by the end of the century.

The third factor was transport. In addition to the river was the Tame Valley Canal, opened relatively late, in 1844, and earlier, George Stephenson's Grand Junction Railway, which cut through Aston in 1837, forever changing the character of this small medieval village.

Between 1831 and 1861 Aston's population rose from 922 to 16,337. During this time railway stations opened at Aston (1854), followed by Witton (1876).

Together with a station at Perry Barr, these transport links opened up the area to even denser urban development, creating a huge demand for sporting activity among local residents, but also for the public of north Birmingham and Staffordshire in general.

The Birmingham region's earliest First Class cricket match took place at the Aston Lower Grounds in 1861. Thereafter, five figure crowds for cricket, athletics, cycling and eventually football matches would be drawn to a purpose built sports ground on Trinity Road, called The Meadow, until it too succumbed to housing developments in 1888 (*see page 48*).

Aston Villa, meanwhile, who started life in 1874 playing informally in and around Aston Park, set up their own ground on a field opposite Perry Barr station on Wellington Road in 1876, and by 1885 were attracting gates in excess of 20,000. They then took over the remnants of the Aston Lower Grounds in 1897, building what would soon become known as Villa Park, of which more later.

But football was not the only commercialised sport to take root in the Tame Valley. In 1928 promoters of the newly imported American sport of greyhound racing opened a track just north of Perry Barr station. A year later the track owners also tried another modern import, called dirt-track, or speedway, racing.

But while speedway has enjoyed only sporadic support in the area, the dogs have stayed the course, as have the runners of Birmingham's best known athletics club, Birchfield Harriers. Despite their amateur status, the Harriers managed to raise funds to build their own stadium across the road from the greyhound track in 1929.

By this time the Birmingham conurbation – having absorbed Aston within its boundaries in 1911 – stretched north to Great Barr, Kingstanding and New Oscott. Radial roads spread their tentacles to Walsall and Sutton, while that most inspired of local transport routes, the Outer Circle bus, linked a network of grounds laid out in the 1920s by companies such as Kynoch's of Witton and Ansells »

▲ Perry Barr viewed from the east in 1937. In the top left is the original **Perry Barr Greyhound Stadium** (1928–84), just in front of which can be seen the tree-lined banks of the River Tame. Beyond this are the **Perry Hall Playing Fields** (in the top left corner of the photograph, beyond the stadium).

In the centre lies the original **Alexander Stadium**, opened in 1929 by **Birchfield Harriers**. The venue is still in use today, having been converted into a dog track when the earlier greyhound stadium was closed in 1984 to make way for the One Stop Shopping Centre.

In the lower right can be seen a corner of **Ansells'** sports ground, one of at least five works grounds to have been laid out in the vicinity (*see Chapter Eight*).

The original Perry Barr Greyhound Stadium seen in the mid 1930s (*top*), and the current greyhound stadium (*above*), showing how open fronted grandstands and turf tracks have given way to enclosed stands and sand tracks in the modern era. Following the stadium's purchase in 2003 by the Greyhound Racing Association (which also owns Hall Green), some £3 million has been spent on revamping and extending the stands to the designs of the Weedon Partnership. Perry Barr's current capacity is 2,000.

>> Brewery, based at Aston Cross, both of whom established sports facilities in Perry Barr, and Joseph Lucas, whose grounds at Moor Lane are now run by the University of Central England (*see Chapter Eight*).

As we shall elaborate upon in Chapter Ten, the area is also characterised by several large expanses of water, popular for boating and fishing. These include Perry Park Reservoir, Witton Lakes, Brookvale Park (where there was an open air swimming pool from 1909–26) and Salford Park, home to a cycle track from 1951–97.

Since 1972 the Tame Valley landscape has been dominated by the overwhelming presence of Spaghetti Junction and the A38 urban motorway, slicing its way through Aston and Witton more brutally than the railway ever managed.

Equally divisive was the widening, also in the 1970s, of Birchfield Road, effectively creating a concrete barrier between Aston and Lozells.

Despite these interventions, Tame Valley's sporting character has remained remarkably intact. Though dominated by three stadiums, Villa Park in particular, numerous community clubs for football, cricket, rugby, bowls and sailing still operate. Despite the incessant background roar of traffic, there are even pockets of genuine tranquility.

Thus the River Tame may itself figure little in people's consciousness – narrow and partly culverted as it is – but the landscape through which it winds has a heritage no less important to Birmingham sport than the rather more obvious, leafier charms of Edgbaston and Bournville.

1. **Birmingham High Performance Centre** (2003–)
2. **Alexander Stadium** (1978–)
3. **Perry Hall Playing Fields** (1929–)
4. **former Perry Barr Greyhound Stadium** (1928–84)
5. **Aston Villa football ground, Wellington Road** (1876-97)
6. **former Alexander Stadium** (1929–78)/**current Perry Barr Greyhound Stadium** (1984–)
7. **Ansells sports ground** (c.1920s–1997)/**UCE** (1997-)
8. **Holford Drive Playing Fields**
9. **Kynoch's/IMI sportsground** (c.1925–2002) (*see page 80*)
10. **Broomfield cricket ground** (c.1880s–c.1913)
11. **Hercules Cycles sports ground** (c.1913–59)/**Aston Villa training ground** (1959–65)
12. **Aston Unity cricket and football ground** (c.1881–1908)/**King Edward VI Grammar School, Aston** (1908–)
13. **Excelsior cricket and football ground** (c.1870s–1890s)
14. **Great Pool/Aston Park** (built over c.1850s–1890s)
15. **Aston Park** (public use 1858–)
16. **The Meadow** (1858–88)
17. **Staffordshire Pool/Lower Grounds boating lake** (built over c.1890)
18. **Aston Lower Grounds cycle track** (1889–97)/**Villa Park** (1897–)
19. **Serpentine fairground site** (c.1900–69)/**Aston Events Centre** (1980–)
20. **Salford Park cycle track** (1951–97)
21. **Salford Park lake** (1919–)
22. **GEC/Magnet Centre sports ground** (c.1920–)
23. **Brookvale Park lake/open air swimming pool** (1909–26)
24. **Witton Lakes** (1926–)
25. **Lucas sports ground** (c.1930–1984)/**UCE** (2003-)

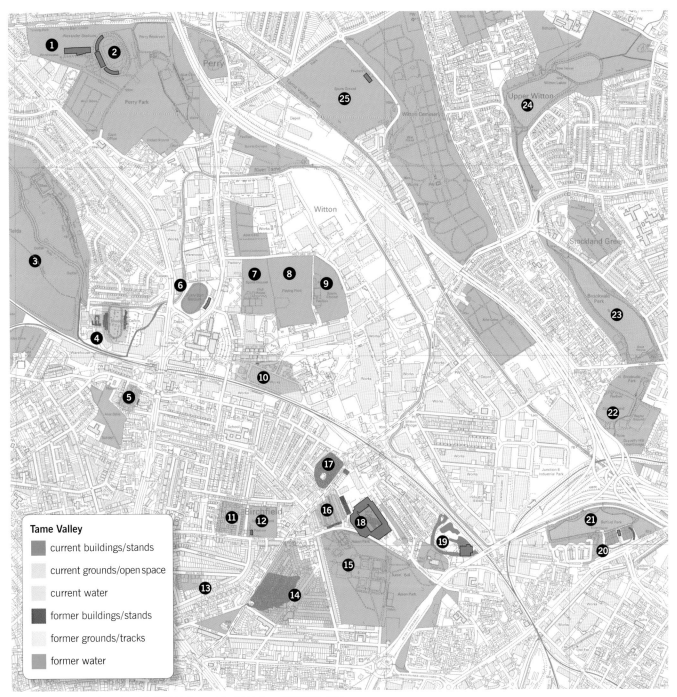

Tame Valley

- current buildings/stands
- current grounds/open space
- current water
- former buildings/stands
- former grounds/tracks
- former water

THE ALEXANDER SPORTS GROUND

Amount spent on Ground - - - £12,225
Amount of Debt at Aug 31st, 1936 - £1,149
Amount Cost for upkeep of Ground and carrying on the work of the Club - £1,000

THE PAVILION

VIEW OF STAND FROM ARENA

Birchfield Harriers' Alexander Stadium, built on 14 acres of land previously used by local power stations for tipping ash, was Britain's first provincial athletics stadium to be owned and managed by an amateur club. Opened on July 27 1929 at a cost of £12,000 and named after WW Alexander – who joined the Harriers in 1880, three years after their formation, and served as honorary club secretary until his death in 1933 – the stadium had a single stand seating 1,000, plus terracing along the home straight and poplar trees at both ends to act as windbreaks.

▲ **Birchfield Harriers** moved to pastures new in 1978, but their emblematic leaping stag and inspiring motto, 'Fleet and Free', continue to adorn the unassuming brick façade of their former home, the original **Alexander Stadium**, situated on a tongue of land sandwiched between Aldridge Road and Walsall Road.

Since forming in 1877, after a dispute over the organisation of a cross country race staged by the Excelsior Club in Aston, Birchfield Harriers have groomed many of England's leading athletes, for example Joe Blewitt, Peter Radford, Ian Stewart, Geoff Capes, Denise Lewis and Ashia Hansen.

But the club also has a long history of innovation. For example,

in order to offset the stadium's running costs the club hired out their facilities for dirt-track racing, initially by the Sunbac Speedway Club of New Zealand.

Shortly before the 1948 London Olympics, an afternoon athletics meeting overran, and so the club decided to switch on the track side lighting that had been installed for speedway. The effect was so spectacular that the following autumn the Harriers initiated Britain's first ever series of floodlit athletics events. Top internationals such as the famed Olympian, Fanny Blankers-Koen, were soon signed up to appear at the Alexander Stadium. One such meeting in the early 1950s drew an impressive crowd of 14,000.

These meeting continued until 1967, by which time dwindling interest, the loss of speedway and mounting running costs forced the Harriers to enter negotiations with the city council in order to find ways of staying in the area, but without the burden of running what was now an outdated arena.

The result, a year after the club's centenary, was a move to a new council-owned track (see *opposite*), half a mile away on Walsall Road.

At this point the old Alexander Stadium seemed doomed, until in 1984 it really did go to the dogs. Or rather, the dogs came to the stadium, after the neighbouring greyhound track had been redeveloped as the One Stop Shopping Centre.

▲ Precious few athletics meetings, in Britain or overseas, nowadays attract sufficient audiences to merit the construction and maintenance of stadiums dedicated solely to the sport. On the other hand, athletes need to train for major events.

Perry Barr's **Alexander Stadium** is therefore typical of a number of publicly-funded British venues – such as London's Crystal Palace, Sheffield's Don Valley Stadium and the Manchester Regional Arena – in that for most of the year its stands lie idle, while its track and indoor training facilities are in daily use.

Located next to Perry Reservoir, alongside the Tame Valley Canal and M6 motorway, the second Alexander Stadium was designed by the City Architects Department and opened on 11 June 1978, when Birchfield athletes ran from the old stadium to their new home bearing Olympic-style torches.

At that stage there was a main stand, seating 3,000 spectators.

To this has been added the curving Nelson Stand (named after former Birchfield athlete and leading women's coach Dorette Nelson), in 1983, and the almost identical Knowles Stand (named after the local politican and former Lord Mayor, Sir Richard Knowles), in 1986.

Since then the Alexander Stadium has staged annual national and international meetings. And yet, ironically, Birmingham's prime athletics event has been, since 1992, the annual IAAF Grand Prix, which draws capacity crowds to the National Indoor Arena.

This emphasis on indoor track and field has been mirrored at Perry Barr, where the £3.3 million **Birmingham High Performance Centre** (*above left*), designed by the City Council's Urban Design Team, was opened with a record breaking 100 metre sprint by the Birchfield Olympian, Mark Lewis-Francis, in February 2003.

Apart from its excellent training facilities – which form part of a national network of centres run by the English Institute of Sport – the building features photovoltaic, or solar powered, cells on its roof for greater energy efficiency.

Undoubtedly a factor in helping to secure for Birmingham the right to host the 2007 European Indoor Athletics Championships – again at the NIA – the High Performance Centre and its adjoining track will no doubt be in demand by foreign athletes visiting for the 2012 London Olympics.

That said, it would seem unlikely that the stadium's seating capacity will need to be increased in the forseeable future, and should the city proceed with a bid for a future Commonwealth Games, this would almost certainly require the construction of a flagship stadium elsewhere in the city.

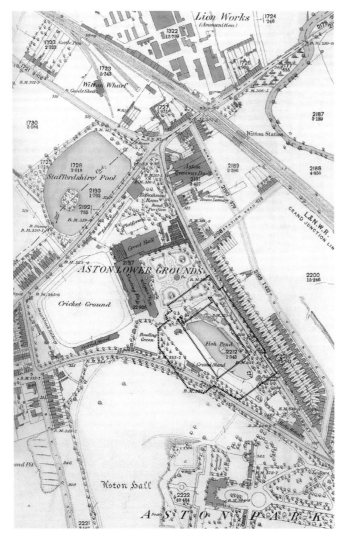

A hand-tinted Ordnance Survey map of the Aston Lower Grounds, dated 1888, with The Meadow marked as 'cricket ground'. Nelson and Jardine Roads were built on the site in 1889. An outline shows the location of the current Villa Park, on what was then the ornamental lake. Note the Lion Works of George Kynoch, one of Villa's early patrons.

◄ From 1864 to 1888, the **Aston Lower Grounds** formed a focus for sport and recreation the like of which has never been known in Birmingham, either before or since.

Refined Edgbastonians may have delighted in their exclusive Botanical Gardens, opened in 1832, while more rumbustious tastes were catered for at the Vauxhall Gardens, in Duddeston (*see page 92*), where cock-fighting and bowls were on offer. But Vauxhall closed in 1850, and for anyone lucky enough to have visited the Great Exhibition in Hyde Park the year after, it was clear that Birmingham was ripe for the latest in popular leisure attractions.

The story of the Aston Lower Grounds is told thoroughly in the centenary history of Villa Park (*see Links*), but for now it is important to relate how this extraordinary amusement park impacted upon sport in the Birmingham area.

That the Lower Grounds were saved from housing development was largely due to Londoner, Henry Quilter, formerly a grocer in New Street before going to work for a building company in Aston. In 1858 Quilter had helped to organise the visit of Queen Victoria to celebrate the opening of Aston Park to the public.

With his love of horticulture and architecture, Quilter persuaded the Lower Grounds owners to let him transform what was then a wilderness – the remains of Aston Hall's kitchen garden and fishing lake – into a paying proposition.

Sport would soon become a crucial part of his business.

Described by the ammunition manufacturer, the Scot George Kynoch – who established his Lion Works in Witton in 1862 – as the 'Magnificent Meadow', the sports ground laid out by Quilter on Trinity Road staged the region's first recorded First Class cricket match, featuring the eminent George Parr and John Wisden, in 1861.

In the 1870s Quilter's sons set up the Birmingham Cricket and Football Club, which in 1875 became a founder member of the Birmingham and District Football Association, along with Calthorpe FC and Aston Villa.

But the enterprise really took off in 1878 when Quilter joined with five co-directors to establish the Lower Grounds Company, with capital of £100,000 and, over the next two years, built a range of substantial pavilions and a Great Hall to dazzle the public.

Designed by architect Thomas Naden, these exotic structures, with their Byzantine-style red brick detailing and ornate central tower, overlooked gardens on the Witton Lane side, and across the now modernised Meadow on the other.

Among the new attractions on offer were a roller skating rink, two lakes (one for boating, the other ornamental), a theatre, an aquarium, menagerie and polar bear house, a switchback railway and toboggan slide, together with cafés, restaurants and the Holte Hotel and its bowling greens.

Add the allure of electric light, a mineral water manufactory and the newly accessible Aston Hall in the adjoining park – all within an easy stroll of Witton station – and there was what one local reporter described as 'the most recherché place of resort in England today'.

From then on, thanks to some hard bargaining with the city's sports clubs, Quilter's Meadow become the Wembley of the Midlands. In 1878 it staged the city's first ever floodlit football match. There were cricket matches featuring Warwickshire from 1882 onwards, as well as the visiting Australians, meetings of the Birchfield and Moseley Harriers, regular cup ties involving the region's leading football clubs and FA Cup semi-finals, in 1884 and 1886. Buffalo Bill's Wild West Circus also made an appearance, while the Amateur Athletics Association's annual championships in 1881 attracted over 10,000 spectators to see two American runners perform – much to the chagrin of the rival Bournbrook Grounds on Bristol Road, whose owners snootily decried the Lower Grounds as 'a sort of tea-garden business'.

In fact, they had a point. Despite attracting nearly 900,000 visitors in its first two years, Quilter went bust after only three years, with The Meadow eventually sold for housing in 1888. But even then the sport continued, for with the gardens now in decline, a new sports ground was laid out on the site of the ornamental lake.

Opened in 1889, the new Lower Grounds was Birmingham's first purpose-built stadium, with a cycle and athletics track, football pitch and banking for spectators.

It was this ground that Aston Villa, at the peak of their success as winners of the League and Cup 'Double', took over in 1897, redeveloping it into Villa Park. Naden's pavilions became the club offices and a gymnasium, and would remain virtually intact until the 1950s. The last remnants were finally demolished in 1981.

Lost too, by 1966, were the site's two bowling greens, so that today all that remains of the Lower Grounds is the Holte Hotel, which had been rebuilt in 1897 and is now owned by Aston Villa, but lies unused and derelict, its future desperately uncertain.

Shown in 1900, three years after Villa converted it into their club offices, Thomas Naden's restaurant and aquarium block (*left*) illustrates the characteristic style of the Aston Lower Grounds during its short but eventful life. The single storey building on the left served for many years as the caretaker's house. Below is the magnificent Trinity Road Stand at Villa Park, designed by the Scottish football ground engineer, Archibald Leitch between 1914–24, and demolished in 2000. For the full story of how the stand nearly bankrupted the club, yet was widely loved and admired by football fans, see *Engineering Archie*, an earlier title in the *Played in Britain* series (*see Links*).

▲ Viewed from the south east, the 43,000 capacity **Villa Park** dominates the local landscape as Aston Hall (*in the foregound*) and Aston Church (*lower right*) did in pre-industrial times. When Aston Villa took over the site in 1897 they rented seven acres. By 1997 they owned 47 in total.

Villa were one of at least eight clubs to have formed in the area during the 1870s. Another was Aston Unity, who played at the Trinity Road grounds (*top left*), now used by **King Edward VI School, Aston**. Also visible, beyond the now cleared site of the IMI factory (formerly Kynoch's), are the playing fields on Holford Drive, Perry Barr.

Two pubs in the vicinity recall the area's former character. These are the **Upper Grounds**, on Trinity Road (*opposite lower*), and, at the apex of Trinity Road and Witton Lane, the now derelict **Holte Hotel**, a popular venue in its own right until the 1960s, for bowls, billiards and darts championships.

Villa Park is today almost a completely new stadium, its oldest part being the 1977 North Stand (*furthest from the camera*). On the right is the Doug Ellis Stand, whose construction in 1995 required Witton Lane to be shifted sideways. Facing the camera is the Holte End, featuring a dubious red brick pastiche of the former Trinity Road frontage, while the new Trinity Road Stand, opened in 2001 with its vast steel-framed cantilevered roof, awkwardly spans Trinity Road at its southern corner (*opposite*).

There may be at Villa Park, to borrow a phrase, a great deal of building but not much architecture. But the stadium remains the city's largest international venue, appropriately perhaps given Aston's role as a cradle of commercialised sport in the Victorian era.

▲ Birmingham's racing cyclists were distraught when Aston Villa removed the cycle track from Villa Park in 1914 in order to increase the ground's capacity. There had been cycling at the Lower Grounds since 1889, eight years before Villa moved in, and before that a more basic track at The Meadow.

To remedy this situation, albeit several decades later – by which time the late Victorian and Edwardian boom in cycle racing had passed – in 1950 Birmingham City Council hired Harry W Weedon & Partners, better known for their Odeon cinema designs, to draw up plans (*as shown above*) for a new track at **Salford Park Lake**, formerly Aston Reservoir, on the banks of the River Tame.

The intention was for Salford Park to complement a more grandiose velodrome proposed for a site in Stechford.

Built at a cost of £12,000 and opened in 1951, the new Salford Park track measured 440 yards, with modest 15 degree, 6 foot high asphalt banking.

Several records were broken here, including Trevor Bull's standing start mile of 1 minute 58.7 seconds (registered in July 1966), which remains unbeaten as of 2006.

As it happened, the Stechford scheme was aborted – a swimming pool was built instead (*see page 141*) – and after further plans to upgrade Salford Park as part of Birmingham's bid for the 1982 Commonwealth Games were also abandoned, the track was finally, and controversially, closed by the City Council in 1997.

Since then the site has been redeveloped for five-a-side football, forcing local cyclists to relocate once again, this time outside the city, to the nearest available track, in Halesowen.

Chapter Five

Sutton Park

On the southern approach to Sutton Coldfield, The Cup Inn – whose current building dates from 1900 – is said to derive its name from a silver cup presented in 1846 by a Mr George Richmond Collis to a jockey called Frost, whose mount 'Auld Squire' won a race at the Holly Knoll racecourse. Holly Knoll was the first of three racecourses in the Sutton Park area during the 19th century. Close by is the Horse and Jockey pub, on the corner of Jockey Road.

Of all the great open spaces of urban Britain – the likes of Hampstead Heath, Heaton Park, Roundhay Park, Town Moor and Holyrood Park – none is larger than Sutton Park.

A mere three miles north of Spaghetti Junction, this 2,400 acre (971 hectares) expanse of woodlands, heathlands, wetlands, marshes and eight man-made pools, is a Site of Special Scientific Interest, a National Nature Reserve and is on English Heritage's Register of Historic Parks and Gardens.

Measuring some eight miles around its outer perimeter, it is also, with some two million visitors a year, one of the Midlands' most popular centres for sport and recreation.

Indeed it could be said that 'sport' – in the original sense of the word – is partly the reason Sutton Park has survived the spread of bricks and mortar.

Here, traversed by the Roman Road, Icknield, or Ryknield Street, was a forested deer park established from 1126 onwards by succeeding Earls of Warwick, the

boundaries of which can still be seen in various banks and ditches in the Holly Knoll, Hill Hurst and Bracebridge Pool areas of the park (and which are now designated as a Scheduled Ancient Monument).

So impressed was Henry VII by the richness of the estate when he passed through in 1485 (en route to the Battle of Bosworth), that in 1489 Sutton Chase, as it was then known, acquired the status of a royal manor.

But the most important date in the park's history is 1528. It was in this year that public access was finally permitted, when Henry VIII – persuaded by his friend and confidant, the Sutton-born Bishop Vesey – granted the town of Sutton a Royal Charter and handed over to the townspeople the whole chase, including the deer park, in perpetuity.

Most of the park would continue to be managed for timber and livestock, although

fox hunting continued from c.1775 until as recently as 1970 (under the auspices of the South Staffordshire Hunt). However the earliest attempts at landscaping for purely aesthetic reasons were made around 1800, when a glade was cut through Holly Hurst in an attempt to offer a distant prospect of the town, accompanied by rustic bridges and an ornamental walk.

Elsewhere in the vast park were several secluded areas where illegal activity could prosper, not least poaching and, during the late 18th century, prize-fighting contests, some of which attracted significant crowds.

Also popular was horse racing. After informal races in the 1830s, two courses were laid out: from 1844–50, by Holly Knoll, and from 1868–79, at Longmoor Valley (*see map on page 55*). A third course, beyond the park's boundaries, in Four Oaks Park, operated from 1881–89 (*see page 56*)

Pleasure cruises were once a regular attraction at Sutton Park, this 30 foot motor launch 'Crusader' being operated by a Mrs Townshend from Blackroot Pool until the 1930s. There were also 50 smaller boats and canoes for hire at Wyndley Pool. Today only Powell's Pool is used for boating, by the Sutton Sailing Club.

Mʳ C TOWNSHEND'S MOTOR LAUNCH, BLACKROOT POOL. SUTTON PARK.

Meanwhile, the opening of the Birmingham to Sutton Coldfield railway line in 1862, helped turn the park into a favourite destination.

So popular indeed that partly to prevent the sheer weight of visitor numbers from damaging the parkland, Sutton's council – no doubt mindful of Henry Quilter's efforts at the nearby Aston Lower Grounds (*see Chapter Four*) – accepted an offer from a Perry Barr market gardener, Mr Job Cole, to create an attraction on a 30 acre site close to the town.

Opened in 1868, the Royal Promenade Gardens were extended in 1879 by the addition of a large domed conservatory, commonly referred to thereafter as the Crystal Palace.

A contemporary report noted 'ample provision has been made for the amusement of visitors. There are boats for sailing and rowing, canoes for paddling and punts for patient fishermen on Wyndley Pool which adjoins the gardens.'

Additional attractions included a hotel, bowling green, archery and croquet lawns, along with a near half-mile bicycle track, in the centre of which was 'one of the best cricketing grounds in the district'.

For courting couples there were also 'shady avenues for "spooning purposes"'. Aston Lower Grounds advertised itself similarly.

Unlike the Lower Grounds, however, Sutton Park was large enough to cater for a much wider cross section of society. As a later guide of 1893 stated, 'of recent years there is an increasing desire for healthful change and life-renewing recreation... in all classes of society, whether it is the retired merchant or the toilers in the great towns of the Midlands...'

Sutton's Royal Promenade Gardens were to prove remarkably long-lasting. A small zoo, funfair and miniature railway were added in the early 20th century. Only in 1962, when the lease expired – by which time the Crystal Palace itself had been demolished – did the gardens finally go out of business. Since then all traces have disappeared, with the site now occupied by Wyndley Leisure Centre and Clifton Road Youth Centre.

After horse racing, the next sport to find a settled home in Sutton Park was golf. This was first played informally close to the Town Gate in the early 1880s, followed by a nine hole course laid out adjacent to the Crystal Palace in 1889. Players wore scarlet coats in order to alert passers-by that a game was in progress.

A permanent private course was then laid out on the north west, or Streetly side of the park, in 1891, where it remains today. For 'toilers' and 'artisans', a more affordable public course was added on the Boldmere, or southern, flank in 1936.

Bordering the Boldmere course is Powell's Pool – at 35 acres the largest of Sutton's eight pools – formed by dams specifically to supply water power to various mills from the early 15th century onwards. It was named after William Powell, who kept a 'spade mill' where he started the manufacture of gardening tools in the mid 18th century.

There was also a button polishing mill at Blackroot Pool, plus other mills for processing leather, making blades and bayonets and, briefly, cotton.

None of these mills was able to survive in the modern era, the

Built between 1970–74, the **Wyndley Leisure Centre features a multi-purpose sports hall, squash courts, a 400 metre athletics track, all-weather five-a-side football pitches, a cricket pitch and a 33 metre indoor swimming pool, Birmingham's largest. Canoeists can train in the pool, but no longer in Wyndley Pool itself, which is now a nature reserve.**

▼ The charming, though now much altered, clubhouse of **Sutton Coldfield Golf Club** was designed by the Birmingham architects Cossins, Peacock and Bewlay in 1897, six years after the club's new Streetly course was opened.

The club itself is the oldest in the Birmingham area, having formed in 1889 on the east side of the park (*see map opposite*), while the course is noteworthy for three reasons. Firstly, it encompasses the Roman Road. Secondly, the clubhouse is not located on the course but on the west side of Thornhill Road. To reach the first tee members must therefore cross what is now a rather busier road than the rural lane depicted in this Edwardian postcard. In doing so they also cross from Staffordshire into the West Midlands.

Finally, the course was redesigned in 1924 by one of golf's leading architects of the early 20th century, Dr Alistair MacKenzie.

Two miles south is the **Boldmere Golf Course**, on Monmouth Drive. Laid out in 1936, Boldmere is one of seven municipal courses within the boundaries of Birmingham, a figure unmatched by any other English metropolitan authority.

» last, on Longmoor Pool, finally closing c. 1900, and the pools are now used mainly for recreation.

During the late 19th and early 20th century they were popular for skating, with cheap rail tickets even offered to encourage more people to take to the ice. Curling was also staged regularly on Wyndley Pool until at least 1914.

Nowadays, fishing takes place on Powell's, Keeper's, Blackroot and Bracebridge Pools, while Powell's is also used for sailing. Until March 2002, Keeper's Pool was also the site of Birmingham's last surviving open air public swimming pool (*see page 58*).

One major aspect of Sutton Park's recreational life has been the staging of numerous mass gatherings: pageants, firework displays, royal celebrations and, most notably, the scouting movement's World Jubilee Jamboree, when 31,000 scouts from 85 countries camped in the park in August 1957. Nearly one million visitors attended, including the Queen.

In December 1972 a further 20,000 spectators gathered for a Special Stage of the RAC Rally. Though organisers considered it

highly successful, the Friends of Sutton Park thought otherwise, concerned at the effect that 130 high speed cars and thousands of rally followers were having on the park's environment. Nonetheless, the race returned regularly until the rally organisers dropped the Midlands from their schedules in the mid 1990s.

Motorised sporting activity does still take place in the park, however. At its highest point, overlooking Longmoor Pool, is 'the flying field', where members of the 200 strong Sutton Park Model Aero Club gather several times per week. Although the club formed around 1980 it is believed that the first model planes were flown in the park as early as the 1920s. (Radio controlled versions were introduced around 1950.)

Following local government reorganisation, in 1974 the Royal Town of Sutton Coldfield, and the park, fell under the jurisdiction of Birmingham City Council, a move deeply unpopular with most local residents. Not only that but the charging of entry fees to the park, introduced for all non-Sutton residents in 1863, came to an end.

With free access for all now restored, the Council's park managers face a delicate balance between ensuring that visitors can enjoy the park's benefits without harming its natural resources.

Sport continues to be a major part of that balance, not least a regular programme of national cross country, road running and cyclo-cross events, pony club rallies, orienteering and charity 'fun runs'.

Hunting may therefore have ceased, but there is still plenty of chasing to be done on this wide and wonderful wilderness on Birmingham's northern edge.

1. **Sutton Coldfield Golf Club** (1891–)
2. **Rifle range** (c.1870s–1918)
3. **Longmoor Valley racecourse** (1868–79)
4. **Longmoor Pool** (1735–)
5. **Boldmere Municipal golf course** (1936–)
6. **Powell's Pool** (c.18th century–)
7. **Model aeroplane 'Flying Field'** (c.1920s–)
8. **Wyndley Pool** (c.1422–)
9. **Wyndley Leisure Centre** (1971–)
10. **Royal Promenade Gardens/ Crystal Palace amusement park** (1868–1962)
11. **Site of first golf course** (c.1882–92)
12. **Keeper's Pool** (c.15th century–)
13. **Keeper's Pool open air swimming pool** (1887–2002)
14. **Holly Knoll racecourse** (1844–50)
15. **Blackroot Pool** (1757–)
16. **World Jubilee Jamboree site** (1957)
17. **Four Oaks Tennis Club** (1906–)
18. **Four Oaks Park racecourse** (1881–89)
19. **Bracebridge Pool** (c.1419–)
20. **Little Bracebridge Pool** (c.1419–)

Sutton Park

current buildings/stands

current grounds/open space

current water

former buildings/stands

former grounds/tracks

The Golf House, Streetley near Sutton Coldfield.   "Scott" Series No. 621.

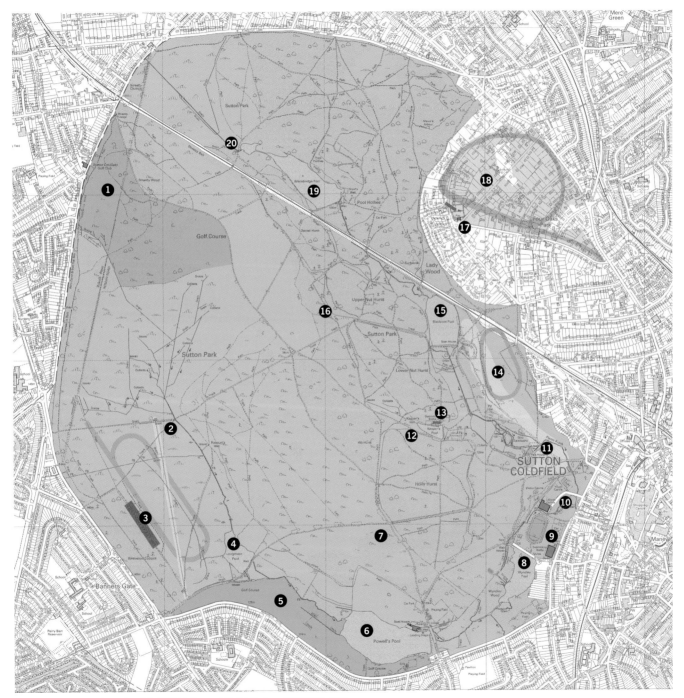

▲ Despite the grandeur of its stands, shown here in the 1880s, **Four Oaks Park Racecourse** enjoyed a lifespan lasting a mere eight years.

To the ire of certain townsfolk races were first held on the west side of the park in the 1830s, on a site (not identified) 'of the most confined and dangerous description, over which it was impossible to let a horse of any value run, even had there been the inducement of good stakes…'

A much improved mile-and-a-half course was then laid out at Holly Knoll, in 1844. Costing £1,000, it occupied an area to the immediate east of Blackroot Pool. By 1850 the *Birmingham Journal* reported the course as being 'well covered with human beings of every class – a greater number never before seen at Sutton'.

Yet by August that same year the course had closed and its stand and other effects sold at auction.

Part of the course can still be detected where it curves through a cutting on the north side of Holly Knoll, while also visible are two raised banks from which spectators were able to follow the action.

No trace survives of the third Sutton course, opened in 1868. Longer than Holly Knoll, and over a mile from the newly opened Sutton Coldfield railway station, its proximity to Longmoor Pool made the going so heavy that racegoers soon dubbed it the 'Morass'.

Nevertheless Longmoor Valley was the area's most popular course yet. Fred Archer, the greatest jockey of the century, rode 21 winners there before local opposition finally forced its closure in 1879. One local reporter complained of the

'bad behaviour of begging children, half naked like Zulus, throwing Katherine wheels into the road'.

No such restrictions would hamper the Clerk of the Course, John Sheldon's next venture. This time he moved to the neighbouring estate of Four Oaks Hall, built in 1712 by Lord Ffolliot but by then in the hands of Sir John Hartopp.

Sheldon paid Hartopp £60,000 for the 246 acre estate, sinking a further £40,000 into the course, as seen above, before its opening in 1881. But despite initially attracting crowds of up to 20,000, and with handsome prize money drawing quality fields, in common with its contemporary speculative venture, the Aston Lower Grounds, Four Oaks never paid its way and was ignominiously closed in 1889.

Both the estate and racecourse were auctioned and replaced

by some of the largest private mansions of Birmingham's business elite. (The Hall itself, empty and dilapidated, survived until 1908.)

The land on which Four Oaks Park racecourse briefly lay is now covered by Bracebridge and Ladywood Roads, with Hartopp Road following the line of the track, while the site of the impressive stands seen here is now the **Four Oaks Tennis Club**.

◀ Curling on **Wyndley Pool** during the freezing winter of 1893.

In common with Association football, curling was a favourite sport amongst Birmingham's Scottish community, one of whose most prominent members was the Aston Villa director and founder of the Football League, William McGregor, seen on the far right.

More recently, this photograph (*below left*) shows the **South Staffordshire Hunt**, gathering at Streetly Gate, Thornhill Road, for their last ever meet in Sutton Park, in 1969, thereby bringing to an end over a thousand years of hunting.

And yet only 50 years earlier fox hunting had been positively encouraged, by the local authority, no less. An Edwardian guide noted that Sutton Park 'rarely fails to provide the necessary wily Reynard' and that 'the fox earths are well looked after by Park employees, the Corporation being desirous of doing all they can to encourage every kind of sport'.

Certain days, the guide went on to say, 'are set aside for rabbiting by the inhabitants'. Also seen regularly until the 1970s were members of the Staffordshire Beagles, out hunting for hares.

Those days may have passed, but the Pony Club of the South Staffordshire Hunt, originally established in 1931, still meets in Sutton Park today.

The site of Sutton Park's once popular open air swimming pool lies exposed on the north bank of Keeper's Pool, shown above from the west in 2005. An enclosed pool had first been provided at this location in 1887, albeit hidden from the public gaze by tall wooden enclosures. As the lido craze swept Britain between the wars, the facilities were then opened up and vastly improved, as seen above right in 1933, and further enhanced in 1961 by the addition of a modern pavilion and café (*right*). After fire ravaged the building in 2002 the facility was finally taken out of commission, leaving Birmingham without a single open air pool for the first time since 1873.

Sutton Park, Keepers Pool, Sutton Coldfield

S.4501

▲ Undeterred by snow or ice, intrepid members of the **Sutton Winter Swimming Club** indulge in their annual Christmas swim at **Blackroot Pool** in 1963, a custom thought to have begun in 1909.

Although the club disbanded in the 1990s, the Christmas tradition is continued today by players and supporters of Sutton Coldfield Rugby Club.

Also still active is the **Boldmere Swimming Club**, formed around 1895, who until the 1920s swam in the deep, and occasionally fatal waters of Powell's Pool. The club has since relocated to the safer environs of the indoor pool at the Wyndley Leisure Centre.

In the foyer is a First World War memorial to fallen members of the Boldmere club, entitled 'Man teaching boy to swim', cast in 1920 by local sculptor Benjamin Creswick. The bronze memorial previously stood on a plinth near the dam at Powell's Pool.

No swimming there nowadays – officially at least – but fishing aplenty, as there also is at Keeper's, Blackroot and Bracebridge pools, which are stocked with bream, carp, perch, pike and tench.

Chapter Six

Moor Pool Estate, Harborne

The sheltered and picturesque waters of the Moor Pool – fed principally by a spring channelled from Lordswood Road – were once frequented by snipes. Since the completion of the surrounding estate in 1912 the pool has been popular for skating, boating and fishing. According to members of the Moorpool Fishing Club, formed in 1967, the pool is best for carp, tench, roach, perch and bream. For non-anglers it is simply a secluded haven.

Stray a few hundred yards north or west from the bustle of Harborne High Street and the townscape changes unexpectedly and quite delightfully.

Redolent of the Garden City movement, the Edwardian Moor Pool Estate is – Bournville notwithstanding – possibly the most charming enclave of 20th century social housing in Birmingham and, arguably, one of the city's best kept architectural secrets.

The estate owes its origins to a proposal to build a tramway from Birmingham to Harborne in 1906. When the scheme failed, a drop in land values along part of the route enabled a group of housing reform advocates – led by the Chairman of Birmingham Corporation's Housing Department, John Sutton Nettlefold – to purchase and develop 54 acres, comprising Poyners and Hill Top Farms, including the Moor Pool itself.

Nettlefold (whose family's screw-making company became part of the Guest Keen and Nettlefold conglomerate in 1902) intended that tenants of the new

development – known originally as City Gardens, and subsequently as the Harborne Tenants Estate – would purchase shares in the company over the years, eventually allowing them to own and manage the estate on a co-operative and democratic basis.

Nettlefold's wife Margaret cut the first sod on October 26 1907, with the first houses becoming occupied in May 1908 and the last of 500 being completed four years later. (Only one house has been added since, c.1970.)

But Nettlefold, a Quaker whose family were related to the Chamberlains, intended to provide more than just housing. As this chapter shows, sporting and recreational amenities were to play an important role in the new estate's social mission. And so they remain, even if other aspects of Moor Pool's founding principles have since been diluted.

Most notably, in 1994 the shareholders (several of whom had acquired considerable property portfolios on the estate) voted to sell their shares to the Bradford Property Trust. Thus

came to an end Birmingham's last self-managed housing estate.

This loss of local control and independence – the estate has since been bought by the Bromley Property Trust – has subtly changed Moor Pool's character.

Although covenants are in place to protect the character of the buildings, and the estate was designated a Conservation Area in 1970, additions such as enclosed porches and plastic windows have multiplied. Meanwhile, as rents have risen and the area has acquired an upmarket reputation, a more transient population has dissipated the sense of community and its resolve to uphold Nettlefold's founding ideals. Whereas houses were once passed from generation to generation and whole families lived as neighbours on the estate, today such a scenario is rare.

That said, the Moor Pool Estate remains a visual delight, constantly throwing up surprises. Indeed it is hard to imagine a more enchanting setting for sport, recreation and sociable living within a modern city.

The Circle serves as the heart of Moor Pool life. There can be found the Estate Management office, billiard room, general store, two tennis courts and Moorpool Hall, run by the residents' association. The Hall houses a large function room and two rare survivors in Birmingham sporting circles, a skittles alley and rifle range.

▶ Viewed from the east, the **Moor Pool Estate, Harborne,** is centred upon The Circle, with its community hall and tennis courts clearly visible. Note also the irregularly shaped green of the Moorpool Bowls Club, lying in a dip between The Circle and the Moor Pool itself, which can just be seen in the foreground, shaded by trees bordering Ravenhurst Road.

That The Circle, the site of the bowls club and the pool were maintained as open spaces for the use of tenants formed an important part of the founder's social mission.

Here, stated the original company directors (each of whom received a maximum £6 annual remuneration), was an environment which offered working people the chance to live 'in clearer air, with open space near their doors, with gardens where the family labour will produce vegetables, fruit and flowers (and) the people will develop a sense of home, life and interest in nature'.

Such amenities, it was added pointedly, would 'form the best security against the temptations of drink and gambling'.

Built at a time when 40 houses per acre were permitted in the city, City Gardens (as the estate was first known) was planned with a density of just nine houses per acre.

High quality building materials predominated, including locally produced red facing bricks and Scandinavian pine. Tenants could choose from nine different house styles, each drawn up by the architects Martin & Martin, although, as at Bournville, minor variations have been incorporated to create added variety.

Similar attention to detail ensured that the roads – several of which followed the routes of existing lanes – were 16 feet wide (enough to allow two hansom cabs to pass), flanked by five foot strips of turf, eight foot wide pathways and tree lined margins.

The Circle originally had at its centre a village green, complete with Maypole, where coronation celebrations, carnivals and firework displays took place. However, during the 1920s the green was replaced by tennis courts, while more recently, many of the areas set aside for allotments have been converted to garage space – ironically perhaps, given that the main road running through the estate is named Carless Avenue. (Not, it might be thought, a piece of visionary town planning by the estate's founders, but in honour of Mary Carless, a noted Harborne benefactor.)

▲ Separated by only a few hundred yards, the Moor Pool Estate has two tennis clubs, each with its own distinctive character.

Laid out in the 1920s on what had been the village green, the two courts of the **Circle Tennis Club** changed from grass to shale in the early 1930s, and, following the defeat of a proposal to build squash courts, to tarmac in the 1980s.

Overlooking the courts are two Grade II listed buildings, the Estate Management Office (*seen above, to the side of the courts*) and Moorpool Hall (*behind the court*), whose ground floor serves as the tennis club's social area. Membership in 2006 stood at around 100 and the club offers regular youth coaching.

Somewhat less well appointed and perhaps less formal is the older **Moorpool Tennis Club** (*right*), at the apex of Margaret Drive and Moor Pool Lane. This was laid out on what had originally been the site of the bowls club, in 1910, during the estate's construction. Its modest timber clubhouse is still the original structure, though considerably extended by the resourcefulness of club members during the 1950s.

▲ Originally located on the site of the Moorpool Tennis Club, the **Moorpool Bowls Club** moved to its present location, nestling in a dip bounded by The Circle, Park Edge and Moor Pool Avenue, in 1913. With them the members brought over their wooden pavilion – the left half as seen above – to which a matching section with flagpole was subsequently added.

In a cupboard within the pavilion (*left*) are stored the members' bowls, or 'woods', several of which are made from lignum vitae, the dense hardwood from which all bowls were fashioned until the introduction of composite materials in the 1930s, yet remains the choice of many bowlers today.

Similarly unchanging is the green's setting, with an assortment of Martin and Martin's distinctive house designs, Moor Pool's generous pathways and the pool itself offering a charming backdrop for the club's crown green players. Passers-by may gain their own enchanting glimpse of the pavilion between the houses, sheds and garages of Moor Pool Avenue.

All this, it should be added, barely 400 yards from Harborne High Street.

▲ Down in the Moorpool Hall basement – known to residents as the Lower Hall or Gymnasium – a member of the **Moorpool Air Rifle and Pistol Club**, formed in 1978, takes aim with his BSA Model D air rifle, believed to date from 1925.

Birmingham-made sporting rifles were once commonly used at the city's numerous shooting ranges, whereas Moorpool's current members prefer pre-charged and spring loaded German guns.

The club also keeps an early 20th century 'bell target', in which a bell sounds when the target is hit.

Although nowadays the idea of using air rifles on licensed premises would be frowned upon, such bell targets were frequently found in shooting galleries attached to Midlands pubs, including two in Harborne – The Vine and The Junction – until the latter decades of the 20th century.

▲ Directly above the current Estate Office, in a former office of the Harborne Tenants Ltd (which had also once been rented out by a tailor), the **Moor Pool Snooker Club** is a relative latecomer to the sporting scene at The Circle, having opened as recently as 1947.

Most of its original fixtures and fittings survive, not least the three mahogany tables and the mahogany and brass marking boards (*left*), supplied by the Birmingham firm of Thomas Padmore & Sons (*see page 107*)

But what really catches the eye, in more ways than one, are the now extremely rare Padmore chalk suspenders, hanging down from the ceiling alongside each table (one of

which is just visible above, to the left of the clock).

With around 70 members, the club opens 364 days per year, from 7.30 each morning, and is run entirely on trust, with each member a keyholder.

While many of the city's snooker clubs charge around £2.00–£2.50 per hour, at Moor Pool members pay a mere 40p per game with no time limit, plus annual fees of just £15. Refreshments are similarly affordable, with tea at 5p and coffee 10p, though members must wash their own cups in the adjoining kitchen.

Note also the original green tiled fireplace at the far end of the snooker room.

▶ Of all the amenities provided at Moor Pool, none is as rare, or as curious as the alley belonging to the **Moorpool Skittles Club**, shown here c.1950. Constructed in the Lower Hall of Moorpool Hall in 1913, shortly after the estate was completed, at a time when regional skittle games were enjoying a revival across England, it is the last known skittle alley in Birmingham and, moreover, probably the last in Britain to feature two alleys – one flat, one crowned – side by side.

Both are 50 feet long and 42 inches wide and are made from maple and oak.

Little is known of why Moor Pool's founders opted for dual alleys, or indeed how common they were elsewhere. Certainly there was a dual alley at The White Swan pub in nearby Harborne Road until the mid 1980s, but both alleys there were flat.

What is certain is that to bowl an 'end' on each alley, as players at Moor Pool are required to do in the course of a match, requires different skills and techniques.

The balls, or 'woods', made from lignum vitae (*right*) are in three sizes (5 inch, 7 inch and 8.5 inch diameter, weighing 3lb, 8lbs and 14lbs respectively), with all but two of the set thought to be the originals from 1913. Unsurprisingly the skittles are less hardy, requiring a new set every decade or so.

Choosing the right wood is crucial. Larger ones scatter the skittles more effectively but even on the flat alley are prone to veer sideways, while the smaller woods run faster, hold their line better, but cause less damage.

Until the mid 1970s, boys from the estate were paid to return the balls and reposition the skittles, or pins, from which practice comes the expression 'earning pin money'.

ROUND ALLEY 30'S	
1921-22	S. NICHOLLS.
1930-31	S. OLDFIELD.
1930-31	R.F. CASH.
1935-36	E. NICHOLLS.
1935-36	S. OLDFIELD.
1936-37	R.F. CASH.
1937-38	G. CLISSOLD
1938-39	R.F. CASH.
1946-47	B.A. FUGGLE.
1947-48	S. OLDFIELD (2)
1947-48	B.C. LAWRENCE
1949-50	B.C. LAWRENCE (2)
1951-52	B.A. FUGGLE
1952-53	B.A. FUGGLE (2)
1952-53	B.C. LAWRENCE
1954-55	B.C. LAWRENCE
1958-59	B.A. FUGGLE (2)
1959-60	B.A. FUGGLE

Over the years the Moorpool Skittles Club has attracted a small but select membership, currently numbering just 25. Moreover, only a handful – most notably the legendary Bert Fuggle – have achieved the ultimate 'Round Thirty' – that is three successive 'strikes' (or 'stacks' as known at Moor Pool) on the Round Alley, worth 30 points. Indeed, not since 1995 has a club member recorded a Round Thirty, and not for want of trying.

Chapter Seven

Stadiums and Grounds

With average gates of 150, the turnstiles of Solihull Borough FC are seldom overtaxed. But in common with around 15 other semi-professional football clubs in the Birmingham area, Borough – based at the immaculate 3,000 capacity Damson Park, opened in 2000 – contribute greatly to the community, offering coaching sessions to local youths and a popular social centre.

Having charted the sporting heritage of five specific districts of Birmingham, we now turn to four thematic studies covering the city as a whole.

Each study focuses on a specific type of 'sportscape', starting with the most visible and high profile type of all, the stadium.

As has been written before in *Played in Britain*, the stadium is as much a part of the urban matrix as a town hall, library or theatre. Stadiums are at the pinnacle of sport's architectural hierarchy; the most ancient in form and the most favoured by governments, politicians and sporting bodies as emblems of power and glory.

Also oft noted is that Britain's stadiums and grounds are mostly in private ownership, and that, as a result, stands have been built as and when funds have become available, using different architects at different periods.

Certainly this is true of all four major stadiums, or grounds – the delineation is often a question of semantics rather than architecture – in the Birmingham area. Despite their status within sporting circles, neither Edgbaston or Villa Park, St Andrew's or The Hawthorns might be described as a 'signature stadium' – that is, one celebrated, at an international level, either for its design or its special heritage.

At the same time, because standing was banned at senior grounds as a result of the 1989 Hillsborough disaster, and because one seat takes the space occupied by two standing spectators, the city's football grounds have all had to grow in bulk, upwards and outwards. Yet despite expanding, each still has a capacity much lower than before.

It might also be said, as is true elsewhere in Britain, that the new all-seated stands, however efficient and profitable, have robbed the city's grounds of their individual character and heritage. The demolition of Villa Park's Trinity Road Stand in 2000 was a particular loss in this respect.

Aesthetics aside, however, it cannot be denied that Edgbaston (opened in 1886), Villa Park (1897), The Hawthorns (1900) and St Andrew's (1906), each exerts a powerful physical and cultural presence within the city's post-industrial landscape.

And of course professional football is by no means the only game in town. Birmingham has a wide network of smaller, comparatively anonymous football and rugby grounds dotted around the suburbs. Several, such as the rugby grounds of Moseley RFC, at Billesley Common, and Birmingham and Solihull, at Sharmans Cross Road, have been laid out only recently, as clubs have been forced either to sell their old grounds in order to stay afloat or to find sites where they may upgrade their facilities. The requirement by certain leagues for grounds to have floodlights has proved particularly problematic for clubs such as Moor Green, based in residential areas.

Conversely, with floodlights and all-weather facilities, social clubs and outreach programmes, the sports grounds of today play a far greater role in community life than in the past. Birmingham may therefore lack a single prominent stadium. But it has grounds enough for modest satisfaction.

Were it not for their lights, many of urban Britain's community-based football and rugby grounds would remain hidden from passers-by. Coles Lane (*right*), the home of Southern League club Sutton Town (the 'Royals') since 1920, is, for example, surrounded by housing and three schools. Spied here from the single access road off Coles Lane is the rear of the main stand, erected in 1956 and seating 250. The ground holds 2,500 overall and also has a rifle range, facilities for table tennis and forms a base for a local sub-aqua club.

▲ Along Tilehouse Lane and Tythe Barn Lane, Shirley, lies a cluster of semi-rural sports grounds, the most established of which is **The Coppice**, home of Midland Combination club **Highgate United FC** (formed 1947).

The Patrick and Philomena Meade Stand (*top*) is, at 97 metres, the longest covered enclosure in Midlands non-league football. Built in 1996, its basic, homespun construction typifies conditions at this community level.

Even simpler, the dug-outs of neighbouring **Wychall Wanderers Juniors FC** (*above*), formed from corrugated panelling and old tyres, have a definite Cubist appeal.

The rapid expansion since 1997 of nearby Dickens Heath has raised fears that this cluster of grounds might fall prey to further housing developments. On the other hand, Wychall Wanderers are now one of the largest junior clubs in the region, with eight teams and over 100 players aged 7-12 years old.

While Aston Villa set up home in a former pleasure palace, in 1906 their rivals Small Heath took over a former brickworks and gypsy camp, bordered by factories, slums and a railway cutting. For the previous 29 years the Heathens had played at a ground on Muntz Street where 35,000 fans had once squeezed in. Now, re-titled as Birmingham FC, they built a ground almost twice that size. A club director served as honorary clerk of works, while a carpenter and former art student, Harry Pumfrey, acted as surveyor and engineer. This image (*right*) taken by Albert Wilkes in 1919, shows Pumfrey's timber Main Stand, which burnt down in 1942 when a fire watchman threw petrol onto a brazier, mistaking it for water.

▲ Until the abolition of standing accommodation as required by the 1990 Taylor Report, the most imposing feature of **St Andrew's** was its **Spion Kop** (named, as were numerous other terraces, after a Boer War battle of January 1900). An estimated 100,000 cart loads of refuse and spoil were used to raise the banking, which, by the time the rear section was roofed in 1931, formed the largest terrace in England. Of the 67,341 fans forming the ground's record attendance in 1939 it is reckoned some 48,000 stood on the Kop.

Photographed here from the Tilton Road End terrace in 1955, the Kop was joined that year by a new **Main Stand** (*above right*), which replaced the ill-fated original (*top*), once post-war building restrictions were lifted. Although austere in amenities and materials, the roof was a comparatively advanced propped cantilever design with five rear columns.

A near identical two-tier stand was built at the Railway End in 1963, but was replaced in 1999. The Main Stand is still in use, however, its lower tier now covered with seats and executive boxes.

Handrail supports at St Andrew's bear the club's initials, and in doing so reflect the local pride that went into the ground's £7.5 million redevelopment during the 1990s. All three new stands were designed by Seymour Harris (architects also of the NEC and stands for West Bromwich Albion), with two other Birmingham firms, Cox Turner Morse and Poole Stokes Wood acting as structural engineers and project managers respectively. St Andrew's, whose centenary falls in December 2006, may yet be superceded by a new stadium in the locality. But it is a compact and atmospheric arena whose redevelopment has been astutely managed.

▲ Wholesale factory clearances and the development of Bordesley Village as part of the Heartlands initiative, have radically altered **St Andrew's** environs since the 1990s. Indeed the ground itself was considered an eyesore until it too was revamped from 1994–99.

Only the 1955 Main Stand (*left*) survives, in what is now an all-seated capacity of 29,949. Though relatively small compared with the club's potential support base, expansion at St Andrew's is limited.

Behind the Main Stand lies an estate of 1920s Flemish-style council flats. The Tilton Road End (*top*) is hemmed in by industrial units (formerly a drop forge, whose hammers were said to have shaken the whole terrace), while the Railway End Stand (*foreground*) is accessible only via bridges over the cutting to its rear. Perched as the ground is on a rise, this stand's rear elevation can be seen from the city centre, yet, as is true of much football architecture, fails to capitalise on that visibility.

But if St Andrew's lacks style, its character does at least reflect the club's status: ambitious, if not quite the finished article.

▲ From the 1960s until 1994 a fibre-glass throstle perched on the scoreboard at the Birmingham Road End of **The Hawthorns**, behind The Woodman Inn. It now occupies a similarly prominent position where two modern stands meet in the opposite corner.

West Bromwich Albion first became known as The Throstles, it is said, either in honour of a song thrush caged at The Plough and Harrow pub – where the team was based during the mid 1880s – or because throstles commonly nested in the area around The Hawthorns.

Albion's other popular nickname, The Baggies, has more contentious origins. A popular theory is that early Albion players wore especially voluminous shorts. But then so did most players in the pre-1914 era.

More plausible is that the term was coined by rival fans, alluding to the loose, baggy overalls worn by local ironworkers who attended Albion's home matches.

▼ Straddling the border between Birmingham and the Borough of Sandwell, **The Hawthorns** is West Bromwich Albion's sixth ground, following their formation – as the West Bromwich Strollers – by workers at the George Salter spring factory in 1879.

Pitches at Cooper's Field, Dartmouth Park and Bunn's Field were used in the early years until, in 1882, Albion leased the Four Acres ground of West Bromwich Dartmouth Cricket Club, whose own football section had disbanded.

Three years later a new site was found on Stoney Lane and it was on this new ground that Albion became founder members of the Football League, along with their local rivals Aston Villa and Wolverhampton Wanderers.

Albion then were a national force. They reached three FA Cup Finals in succession from 1886–88 and faced Villa in a further two, in 1892 and 1895.

But Stoney Lane was a poor ground, rented on a short lease and with a notoriously sloping pitch.

So it was that in 1900 Albion relocated to a 10.5 acre site on Birmingham Road, belonging to Sandwell Park Colliery and served by two pubs, The Woodman Inn and the Hawthorns Hotel.

That the site was a mile from the town centre and barely three miles from Aston Villa's newly opened ground mattered less than its pivotal position on a tram route, on the edge of three densely populated boroughs, West Bromwich, Smethwick and Handsworth.

Unlike St Andrew's, with its Kop, or Villa Park with its Holte End, The Hawthorns did not develop one dominant terrace. Rather, all four sides remained relatively compact.

The Smethwick End, from which this image was taken in 1964, was covered by a wooden Belfast roof in 1904. To the left, the Halford's Lane Stand was developed in

stages between 1914 and 1958. (Inside the stand were some of Britain's earliest electronic turnstile counters, installed in 1949.)

To the right is the Rainbow Stand (named because of its multi-coloured seats), completed in 1964 on what had formerly been called the Handsworth Side terrace. Its old roof was re-erected, as seen here at far end, at the rear of the Birmingham Road End terrace (where the Woodman scoreboard can just be seen behind the Rainbow Stand roof).

The floodlights, identical to those at Villa Park and St Andrew's from the same period, were erected by GEC of Witton in 1957.

None of these structures survive today (not even The Woodman Inn). But the Hawthorns' pitch still slopes, six feet from north to south, three feet east to west. And at 550 feet above sea level, The Hawthorns is also the highest ground in senior English football.

◀ Seen from the east in 2005, **The Hawthorns** has expanded its boundaries as a result of post-Hillsborough modernisation, yet has a much reduced capacity. Whereas it once held a record 64,815 in 1937, today it has 28,000 seats.

The oldest of the four sides is the Halford's Lane Stand (*top*), by Seymour Harris architects in 1981. Both the Birmingham Road Stand (*right*) and Smethwick End Stand (*left*) were designed by the Tim Ralphs Design Group in 1994, followed in 2001 by the East Stand, by Ward McHugh, which now forms the core of the club's activities (the narrower Halford's Lane side being more limited).

Although separated from West Bromwich town centre by the M5 motorway, The Hawthorns enjoys excellent access thanks to the proximity of the Junction One roundabout (*top left*) and The Hawthorns Midland Metro station (*not shown*), first opened in 1931 and reopened in 1995.

On the north side of Birmingham Road, by the motorway junction, can be seen the ground of West Bromwich Dartmouth Cricket Club, which formed in 1834 and moved to its present site, on the edge of Sandwell Park golf course, in 1920. Dartmouth Park itself, visible in the distance (*top right*) staged several early Albion games, and adjoined the football club's Four Acres ground, used from 1882–85.

At the Hawthorns' Birmingham Road entrance stands the **Jeff Astle Gates** (*left*), in honour of Albion's popular centre forward who died in 2002. Designed by Parson Brothers, the gates were financed by the *Grorty Dick* fanzine, the Shareholders For Albion and Boing Internet groups, the Smethwick Regeneration Partnership and the Smethwick Town Team.

▲ While Warwickshire, Villa, Blues and Albion have all garnered sufficient resources to redevelop their own historic grounds, **Moseley Football Club** (formed in 1873 as an offshoot of Havelock Cricket Club), were forced to leave **The Reddings** in May 2000, thus ending 120 years of rugby at this modest, but much loved suburban venue on Reddings Road.

Shown above in 1949 is the ground's West Stand (*left*) and its assortment of stands and pavilions on the east side (*right*). Open terracing occupied both ends of the ground (*see page 2*).

Having played their early games as Havelock FC at St Paul's Road, Camp Hill, and at three other sites (including the grounds of Moseley

Hall), Moseley first leased The Reddings from the Taylor Estate in 1880, for £25 per annum. (The names Upper and Lower Riddings appear on a 1840 Tithe map.) For a while, the players changed at The Trafalgar pub, Woodbridge Road, then took the penny tram (steam or electric) up to Reddings Road.

During its twelve decades as the city's foremost rugby ground, The Reddings staged hockey, was home to Moseley Cricket Club from 1880–1930, and from the 1930s also offered tennis courts behind the Reddings Road end.

The opening of a new clubhouse in 1963 and floodlights two years later presaged a golden era. Seven members of Moseley's 1972–73 side were internationals, while

crowds in excess of 5,000 enjoyed a feast of club, international and representative games, unsurpassed in Birmingham's rugby history.

Success could not be sustained, but ultimately it was Rugby Union's controversial switch to professionalism in 1995 that led to The Reddings' demise.

To compete in rugby's new age, Moseley proposed converting The Reddings to a 5,500 capacity all-seater stadium. Local residents opposed the plans, however (including, ironically, the former Labour Sports Minister Dennis Howell), and with higher costs and dwindling crowds, Moseley slipped into administration in 1998 and were forced to sell the ground to Bryant Homes to pay off debts.

From 2000 Moseley played on at Birmingham University, kept alive by the dedication of members, the goodwill of creditors and support from Birmingham City Council.

Proposals to relocate the club to Oxford in 2003 were thankfully averted, before in September 2005 a new ground was opened at Billesley Common, with temporary stands and a clubhouse. Though lacking character, the site does at least bear a B13 postcode, and forms a base for the club's training programme, which serves over 10,000 schoolchildren in the city.

Meanwhile The Reddings is now covered by housing, on roads called Twickenham and Harlequins Drives – names that have no direct links with the locality or club whatsoever.

Run by Sandwell Leisure Trust, Smethwick's Hadley Stadium opened in May 1962 at a cost of £90,000, on land donated by Sarah Hadley. In 1972 it hosted a GB v. West Germany athletics international, and in 1966 drew a 10,000 crowd to a charity football match. Its 500 seat stand is used today by fans of amateur clubs Sikh Temple FC and Mohal FC.

▶ Supporters, players and officials of Birmingham's most prominent amateur football club, **Moor Green**, gather for the grand opening of **The Moorlands**, Sherwood Road, Hall Green, on October 18 1930.

There might have been a similar celebration for the ground's 75th anniversary, had vandals not set fire to the stand in January 2005, thereby not only destroying one of the most handsome pre-war stands in local football, but also forcing Moor Green – members of the Nationwide Conference North (that is, two divisions below the Football League) – to switch their games to the home of Solihull Borough, three miles eastwards. (Ironically, Solihull had been tenants of Moor Green themselves for nine years, after selling their own ground in 1989.)

As their name indicates, Moor Green were formed in Moor Green Lane, in 1901, by players of the Moseley Ashfield Cricket Club.

Various grounds were used over the years, until in 1930, just as Hall Green was starting to emerge as a suburb in its own right, with wide, tree-lined dual carriageways and large estates of semi-detached houses – not to mention the new greyhound stadium (*see page 75*) – Moor Green's secretary, who was also an estate agent, purchased part of Old House farm, setting aside seven acres for the new Moorlands ground.

In fact, there was space for Moor Green, plus a second football pitch (rented for many years by Highgate United), and a cricket square.

Once terraces were raised around the main pitch, The Moorlands was able to accommodate a record 5,000 crowd for an Amateur Cup tie v. Romford in 1951.

Further proof of the club's status came in 1964, when it paid £6,250 for the freehold.

But progress was to have its drawbacks.

When Moor Green rose up to the Southern League in 1983 they were required to install floodlights, a prospect not to the liking of the club's residential neighbours. In order to limit the levels of light spillage the club therefore turned their pitch by 90 degrees. This, however, resulted in the loss of the second pitch and the main terrace, and meant that the old stand now sat behind the goal, rather than on the half way line.

At the same time, to reduce their impact on the surroundings, the new floodlights had to be mounted on hinged poles and winched upright before use.

Although not ideal, the ground's reorientation did at least give Moor Green hope for the future.

But then came the fire, since when The Moorlands has lain empty and desolate, its future in the balance.

Before the inferno – Moor Green's 250 seat timber stand was designed in 1930 by the club's honorary architect, Wilfred Veal, and cost £1,000. The single storey changing rooms and bars were later additions. After the pitch was moved in 1983 somewhat oddly the stand looked down on the back of a goal, rather than the halfway line, as originally intended.

A crowd gathers at the Alcester Road entrance to the King's Heath greyhound track in May 1939. Owned by the King's Heath Racecourse Company and, as the sign indicates, the home also of a popular horse show every Whit Monday, King's Heath was Birmingham's first greyhound racing venue, having opened in May 1927, three months before Hall Green (*see opposite*) and a year before Perry Barr (*see page 42*). Little remembered today, King's Heath was also the city's first track to close, in March 1971. The site is now covered by housing on Wynfield Gardens and Leander Gardens.

▲ When electrical hare coursing, or greyhound racing, first arrived from the United States in 1926 – in Manchester, to be precise – it spread rapidly around Britain's major towns and cities. Indeed, so alluring was its after-dark blend of track lighting, mechanised hares and Totalisator boards, as at **King's Heath** (*top*), that football's status as the most popular working class sport was seriously questioned during the 1930s.

But as attendances at tracks started to decline from the 1950s onwards, promoters had to work harder to attract higher spending punters. An example of this was the trackside American Bar at King's Heath (*above*) opened in December 1949, with Lloyd Loom furniture and a television behind the bar.

▶ When William Welch sold his Olympia Sportsground in York Road to the newly formed Greyhound Racing Association in 1927, 2,400 residents in this up and coming suburb registered their opposition. Nevertheless, 20,000 onlookers witnessed the new stadium's opening on August 24 that year.

But as this 1929 aerial view of **Hall Green Greyhound Stadium** shows, in addition to the outer turf track for dogs there was an inner cinder track for another new sport.

Like greyhound racing, speedway was thoroughly modern. Staged under lights – at a time when the football authorities remained resolutely opposed to night games – its riders appeared like speed jockeys of the new mechanical age. It was fast, noisy and of course many of the bikes and their components were locally produced, at BSA, Joseph Lucas and Bakelite, all of whose works were within a mile of Hall Green.

Hall Green's speedway licence was eventually revoked in 1937 following the death of a rider.

Another sport to be staged was football. Starting in 1951 Hall Green Amateurs seldom drew crowds of more than 100, but they were strong enough to challenge Moor Green's dominance until their lease was ended in 1965.

In truth the 1960s were tough for greyhound promoters. During the 1930s crowds of 30–35,000 had packed Hall Green. But the advent of television, followed by the legalisation of off-course betting in 1961 led to a dramatic decline and the closure of dozens of tracks.

Hall Green survived because of its densely populated catchment area, and because Birmingham's economic muscle encouraged the GRA to invest over £2.2 million in its modernisation. Firstly, in 1970,

the track was resurfaced with sand and the mechanical Tote Board, built in 1946, was replaced by an electronic version (*top right*).

The Grandstand (*above*), built in phases from 1972–89, features a rooftop hare control box, seating for 360 diners on its enclosed upper tier, and a ground floor concourse packed with bars and betting outlets, leading out onto a paddock holding 2,700 spectators. Opposite, on the former Popular Side, is a second enclosed stand, added in 1987. Hall Green is thus one of the few tracks with viewing from more than one side. It also has its own snooker club and, since 1990, a 48 bed hotel on site.

Racing is held on three evenings per week, attracting crowds in the region of 1–3,000. By today's standards that is success indeed, and helps explain why Hall Green won GRA Racecourse of the Year in 2002.

Moreover, with racing also thriving at Perry Barr, Birmingham is now the only city other than London to support two greyhound tracks – not something even the bravest of punters would have dared bet on 20 or 30 years ago.

Chapter Eight

Works grounds

Having helped to found the Football League in 1888, the Aston Villa director and Summer Lane draper William McGregor became the Birmingham and District Works Amateur Football Association's first president, in 1905. 'Nothing is better calculated to bring about a good understanding between employer and employee...' he wrote in the *Sports Argus* of May 26 1906, 'than for the employer to take a personal and practical interest in the sports and pastimes of those engaged at his factory.'

In common with so many strands of Birmingham's history, the story of grassroots sport cannot be told without reference to the industrial and commercial life of the city. In Birmingham it would seem, work and play were once inextricably linked.

Indeed from the 1920s until the 1970s several of the region's most extensive sports facilities were owned or operated by private companies for the benefit of their employees. In 1955, it has been calculated, at least 94 local works clubs played at their own grounds, whilst with a membership of 254 clubs, the Birmingham and District Works Amateur Football Association was the largest of its kind in the world.

As recounted earlier, until the late 19th century much of Birmingham's manufacturing took place in small workshops concentrated around the city centre. This, combined with long working hours and a shortage of parks and open spaces, meant that for most working people, opportunities for recreation remained limited.

An unidentified works team from the Early Closers League poses at the start of the 1923–24 season. Such leagues were popular amongst workers whose traditional half-day off was Wednesday rather than Saturday. These included staff of Birmingham Tramways, Lewis's department store, bakers, grocers and other retail and self-employed traders.

From 1870 onwards, however, the introduction of early closing on Saturdays brought profound changes in the habits of industrial workers. Not least, sports clubs soon sprang up all over the city.

Studies have shown that some 20–25 per cent of Birmingham's emerging football and cricket clubs during the 1870s and 1880s were based around churches and Christian institutions. Of equal importance was the workplace.

Members of the Birmingham Clerk's Association, for example, set up one of the city's earliest football clubs, Calthorpe FC, while workers from the George Salter spring factory formed the team that would eventually become West Bromwich Albion.

But while there may have been over 20 works-related football clubs by 1880, few companies saw the provision of grounds as part of their wider social remit.

Kynoch's ammunition works (later IMI), established in Witton in 1862, for example, had no

sports facilities until the early 20th century, even though George Kynoch was otherwise a patron of local sport. The Cadburys, by contrast, went to great lengths to include recreation grounds at their new Bournville Works from 1879 (*see Chapter Three*), and were followed by King's Norton Metal Works at Melchett Road and Nettlefolds, who laid out a sports field on the junction of Pershore Road and Fordhouse Lane.

These examples amply showed that sport offered real benefits.

First and foremost, wholesome recreation provided a healthier, stronger workforce, less prone to absenteeism. Sport was character building too, fostering friendship, teamwork and a sense of pride in the company. Not least, Saturday afternoon sport also kept working men away from the public house, for a few hours at least.

But however desirable such aims, most companies could not apply them meaningfully until, around the late 19th and early

20th centuries, they started to follow Cadbury's example by migrating to the city's outskirts, where cheap land, often acquired with future factory expansion in mind, allowed them to develop substantial sports facilities. (Other firms bought or leased grounds on separate sites, or simply hired facilities at weekends.)

By today's standards the sheer scale of provision and level of participation in Birmingham works sport was astonishing.

Certain firms, such as Bakelite (who moved to Tyseley in 1931), and Fisher & Ludlow (who in the 1950s employed 14,000 workers making car panels in Castle Bromwich), had workforces large enough to sustain their own 'in house' football leagues, in addition to competing against outside opposition. Other company teams banded together to form their own specific business leagues: for clerks, or transport workers, for example. There was also a Birmingham Business Houses Cricket Association, and for female employees, a Birmingham Industrial Netball League. Other works teams took part in rugby, bowls, hockey, darts, chess, billiards, snooker, bridge and even tug-of-war.

Of the 94 works grounds identified in 1955, the majority succumbed to developers in the 1960s and 1970s, as the local economy prospered and land values rocketed. Of those that did survive, few then managed to outlive the wholesale factory closures that wiped out nearly half of all manufacturing jobs in Birmingham during the 1980s.

Other grounds, such as at Lucas's on Shaftsmoor Lane, were turned into car parks to cater for employees driving to work.

Bowls aside, no business house leagues operate today, while the once mighty Birmingham and District Works AFA finally threw in the towel in 2000, leaving the few remaining works teams – mainly representing long-established industrial firms, former public utilities and government offices – to make their way in the wider world of regional leagues.

Currently, at least 21 former works grounds survive, of which 12 remain in company hands. Few are of intrinsic interest purely as landscapes, or for their associated buildings. But as reminders of a once extraordinary social phenomenon, and of an age – surely past – when companies went to great lengths to provide sports facilities for their staff, they rank among the most important historical sportscapes in the city.

▲ Hidden from view between Brookvale Park and the elevated section of the M6 motorway, and only yards from Spaghetti Junction, is the **Magnet Centre**, Park Approach, the once proud former works ground of **GEC Witton**.

GEC, who set up their works in the appropriately named Electric Avenue, Witton, in 1900, were amongst the city's most generous providers of sports facilities for their employees. Workers at their other factories in Coventry and Wembley were similarly well provided.

The substantial three storey Magnet Centre itself (*top left*), dating from the early 1920s, housed a large gymnasium, two billiard rooms, a reading room, committee rooms and a dining hall seating over 1,000.

Now partly used as a religious and community centre for

Birmingham's Greek Orthodox community, the centre overlooks a seven acre sports ground, which originally featured pitches for football, hockey and cricket, together with three tennis courts. (Between the wars GEC ran six teams for football, two each for hockey and rugby union, and a club for anglers.)

The grounds are now owned by Birmingham City Council.

▲ To celebrate its Golden Jubilee in 1955 the **Birmingham and District Works AFA** displayed its impressive array of 96 trophies and shields in the window of Lewis's department store on Bull Street. Needless to add, most of them were supplied by local workshops, including the Silversmiths Cup, contested by teams connected with the trade.

At its formation in 1905 the AFA resolved to promote 'wholesome recreation… fostering friendship and promoting goodwill, by healthy rivalry… to assist in the social unity between employers and employed… and to help by recreation to fit men better for their daily task, and make of them more contented workmen'.

Its appeal was immediate, some employers being so keen that they signed up before being able to field a team. When the first league season kicked off in 1906 there were 52 teams. By the following season that figure had tripled, and although the ensuing war and depression would see numbers fluctuate, by 1939 the AFA had grown to become the world's largest works football association, with 278 teams from 205 clubs, competing in 19 divisions.

So large was the organisation during this period that the White Horse Hotel in Congreve Street was block booked for an entire week in order to stage the annual award ceremonies.

At the time of the 1955 Jubilee the AFA's prospects looked bright. Local factories' order books were full. Unemployment was virtually unknown. The advent of a five day working week in the late 1940s also allowed more Saturday morning games, thereby freeing players to watch professional matches in the afternoon.

Yet by 2000 just 10 teams remained, forcing the AFA to fold, five years shy of its centenary.

But not all is lost. A number of the trophies and shields are known to have survived, and it is hoped that these, and surviving AFA records, will be retained and conserved as worthy artefacts of the city's sporting history.

•Abingdon Ecco (later King Dick) joined Association in 1908 •Accles & Pollock 1917 •Acme Works 1928 •Adams Athletic 1920 •Adams & Benson 1926 •Adie Brothers 1912 •HS Adminster 1934 •Aeroplane & Motor Aluminium Castings 1938 •Aga Heat 1936 •Albion Pressed Metal 1952 •Albion Engineering 1919 •Albright & Wilson 1931 •Aldis Brothers 1954 •Henry Allday 1920 •PG Allday 1935 •Alldays & Onions 1917 •Allen Everitt 1923 •Allied Road Transport 1920 •Ansells Brewery 1921 •Arcadians (Wilkinson & Riddell) 1913 •James Archdale 1917 •Arden Hill 1906 •Aremesco 1927 •Argosy Works 1926 •Ariel Motors 1908 •Armstrong Works 1906 •Ash & Co 1919 •F Ashby & Sons 1925 •Ash & Lacy 1923 •HS Ashdown 1933 •Assay Office 1912 •Aston Brass & Whitehouse 1912 •Aston Chain & Hook 1917 •Aston Loco 1921 •Aston Road Tube Works 1935 •Atkinsons Brewery 1922 •W & T Avery 1906 •Auster Athletic 1913 •Austin Aero 1938 •Austin Motor 1906 •Wm Bailey 1934 •Bakelite Sports 1934 •Barker & Allen 1935 •Barker Bros 1906 •Barwell James 1937 •Baskerville Works 1919 •Bathurst Works 1912 •Batteries (Redditch) 1931 •Baxters (Bolts Screws & Rivets) 1935 •Bayliss Wiley 1922 •BEA (Nechells) 1951 •Belgrave Sports (Blackheath) 1943 •Belliss & Morcom 1906 •Bendix Brakes 1933 •Benton & Stone 1907 •James Beresford (Cato St) 1906 •Berkel 1925 •Berry's Electric 1945 •Best & Lloyd 1907 •Bill Switchgear 1947 •Billesley Estates Dept 1936 •Birchley Rolling Mills 1925 •Alfred Bird 1951 •Birfield

Industries 1945 •Birlec Sport 1937 •Birmalium 1911 •Birmid Sports 1937 •B'ham Battery & Metal 1906 •B'ham City Police 1954 •B'ham City Transport (Trams) 1907 •B'ham Estates Dept 1937 •B'ham City Gas 1906 •B'ham Guild 1919 •B'ham LMS 1946 •B'ham PO Messengers (later PO Youth) 1921 •B'ham Parks & Cemeteries 1954 •B'ham Railway Carriage & Wagon 1926 •B'ham Salvage 1922 •B'ham Stopper 1935 •B'ham Telephones 1945 •B'ham Tool & Gauge 1925 •B'ham Water Dept 1937 •Bisley Works 1925 •H Bisseker 1919 •S Blanckensee 1912 •Bloore & Pillar 1935 •Bolton Works 1907 •Booth James (Argyle St) 1919 •Booth James (Sheepcote St) 1928 •Booth Samuel 1937 •Bordesley Junction 1920 •Bournville Aero 1944 •Bournville Athletic 1907 •Bournville Loco 1920 •Bournville Works Housing 1925 •Bowden Brake 1909 •Bowman 1934 •Boxfoldia 1925 •Brades Steel (Wm Hunt & Sons) 1919 •Bradmore 1933 •Braithwaite 1945 •Brampton Bros 1922 •Breedon Works 1906 •T & J Brettell 1935 •Brittania Tube 1908 •Briscoe 1925 •British Autos 1920 •British Brass Fittings 1925 •British Castings 1928 •British Cyanides 1919 •British Hub 1920 •British Industrial Plastics 1936 •British Lighting & Ignition 1920 •British Oxygen 1951 •British Pens 1938 •British Rolling Mills (Brymill) 1938 •British Timken 1929 •British Typewriters 1944 •J Brockhouse 1932 •Bromford Tube Works (Stewarts & Lloyds) 1923 •Brooke Tool Mfg 1935 •Brookes & Adams 1925 •JB Brooks 1909 •J Broughton 1931 •JB Bruce 1907 •Bryant (Builders)

1938 •BSA (Coventry Road) 1920 •BSA Guns (Shirley) 1945 •BSA Motor 1909 •BSA Recreation 1907 •BSA (Sparkbrook) 1920 •BSA Tools 1945 •BTH Recreation (Blackheath) 1927 •Buck & Hickman 1937 •Buckler & Webb 1950 •Bullers (Tipton) 1919 •Bulpitt 1919 •Burman 1936 •George Burn 1954 •Burton Delingpole 1928 •Bushell 1912 •Butlers Sports 1948 •Buttons 1912 •Bywater 1938 •Callender Cable 1925 •Callenders Foundry 1926 •Calthorpe Motor 1912 •W Canning 1929 •Carola Products 1944 •J Cartland 1908 •FA Cartwright 1923 •R Cartwright 1948 •Castle Bromwich Aero 1944 •Central Relay Wireless 1948 •Century Works 1925 •Chad Valley 1931 •Chamberlain, King & Jones 1937 •Chance Bros 1920 •Chance & Hunt 1910 •Charford Athletic (Southalls) 1932 •Thos Chatwin 1907 •Cincinnati Milling Machines & HME 1936 •City Tube Works 1929 •Clarke & Gough 1937 •Clarkson 1920 •Clear Hooters 1950 •Clement (Mudguards) 1938 •Charles Clifford 1919 •Clifford Aero & Auto 1947 •Clifford Covering 1948 •Clifford Motor Components 1947 •Charlesworth Mouldings 1949 •Cobden Works 1908 •Cochrane 1936 •Colemans Athletic 1929 •Coleshill Hall 1938 •Components (Tyseley) 1917 •James Cond 1937 •Constructors 1928 •Coolex 1945 •Coombs Wood Colliery 1921 •Cooper & Goode 1920 •W Cooper 1931 •Copper & Alloys 1949 •Country Homesteads 1938 •Cox & Danks 1938 •Cranes Chemical 1932 •Cranes Screw & Colgryp Castor 1917 •Comalin 1936 •TD Cross 1924 •R & A Crossland 1948 »

◄ As listed in the organisation's Golden Jubilee brochure, between 1905 and 1955 no fewer than 677 companies, works and organisations belonged to the **Birmingham and District Works Amateur Football Association**.

Of the total, 254 were still in membership in 1955, a figure that, according to Sir Stanley Rous, Secretary of the Football Association, did 'great credit to the industrial concerns in the area and to the sporting outlook of their directors. Their consideration for the welfare and recreation of the employees is also demonstrated in the most practical manner by the large number of splendid sports grounds for which they have been responsible.'

To the people of the West Midlands, the list, which continues on following pages, provides a poignant reminder of the region's industrial and commercial past. Few families will have been untouched by at least one of the companies, while much of Birmingham's urban landscape throughout the 20th century was to a large degree characterised by the extent and distribution of their factories, offices and grounds.

In a very real sense the Birmingham and District Works AFA was one of the great social achievements of Birmingham's industrial age.

▲ Despite the modernity of their factories and plant, Birmingham companies reverted, it would seem without exception, to more traditional, vernacular styles for their sports grounds, as typified by the mock-Tudor 1920s clubhouses at **Kynoch's**, **Holford Drive**, in Perry Barr (*top*) and **Dunlop's**, on **Holly Lane** and **Wood Lane**, Erdington (*above*).

The latter, in particular, offered a homely contrast to the nearby Base Stores building, the red brick colossus that was (and still is) Fort Dunlop, completed in 1923 after Dunlop's move from Aston Cross (*see page 104*).

But for all their lack of pretension, clubhouses performed a role that transcended sport. In Birmingham's competitive job market, being able to offer a wide range of sporting and social amenities was vital if a company was to attract a high standard of apprentice. Equally, companies would often treat favourably those applicants who showed particular prowess in sport.

Neither pavilion shown here survives, both grounds having been redeveloped during the last 15 years as industrial parks.

» •Crown Bedding 1953 •Curzon Templars (L & NW Railway) 1920 •CWS (Cabinet Works) 1921 •Cyclo Gear 1935 •Daimler Motors 1923 •Daniel & Arter 1906 •Daniel Mfg 1938 •Edwin Danks (Oldbury) 1913 •Darlington & Simpson 1948 •Dart Spring 1935 •Davenports 1907 •Davis Iron & Steel 1952 •Deakin & Francis 1919 •Delta Metal 1907 •Dennison Watch Case 1912 •Deritend Stampings 1912 •Deykin & Harrison 1913 •Diamond Screw & Cotter 1932 •Diecasting Ltd (Dical) 1928 •District Iron & Steel 1913 •Docker Bros 1934 •Dowding & Mills 1944 •Dudley Road Infirmary 1949 •Thos Dudley 1936 •Dunelt Cycle 1927 •Dunkley Prams 1925 •Dunlop Rubber 1906 •Duport Foundry 1923 •Earle, Bourne 1906 •Ebro Works (Frost & Co) 1933 •A Edmonds 1935 •WP Edmund 1937 •Electric Ignition 1906 •Electro Mechanical Brake 1927 •Electric Ordnance (Stellite Works) 1906 •Electric Supply Dept 1917 •Elkington 1910 •Elliotts Metal 1919 •Ellis & Co 1912 •Alfred Ellison 1936 •Geo Ellison 1919 •J Elewell 1931 •Empyrium Welding & Mfg 1938 •Enfield Cycles 1929 •Ericcson Engineering (Peerless & Ericcson) 1944 •Evered 1907 •Excelsior Works 1907 •Exide Sports 1936 •Farrington Works 1921 •Fearnhill Sports 1935 •Ferris Athletic 1933 •Fields Tilleries 1925 •Filleries Toffees 1926 •Fisher & Ludlow 1921 •Fisher Foundries 1944 •Fletcher Hardware 1924 •FR Ford 1936 •Forward Electric 1931 •Forward Radiator 1933 •Foundry Engineering 1920 •Galvo Sports 1931 •Gaskell & Chambers 1934

•GCF (Blackheath) 1917 •Gear Grinding 1955 •General Electric (Witton) 1906 •General Electric (Ileene Works) 1913 •General Electric (Magnet Works) 1928 •GH & PT United 1944 •F Giles & Sons 1948 •Gills Athletic 1937 •Ginder & Gouch 1912 •Girdex Engineering 1948 •Girling Sports 1944 •Globe Works (Blackheath) 1937 •Glover 1906 •Golf Ball Developments 1933 •HM Grant 1920 •Green 1913 •WW Greener 1920 •Grice, Grice & Co 1929 •Gridway Steel Construction 1950 •Griffin Foundry 1936 •AE Griffiths 1935 •Grosvenor Workman 1907 •Great Western Railway Sports 1909 •Halesowen Steel Works 1912 •Halford Cycles 1935 •Hall Green Foundry 1920 •Hall St Rolling Mills 1925 •Hallidays Drop Forgings 1936 •Ham, Baker & Co 1919 •JG Hammond 1925 •Hams Hall Electric 1938 •Hamstead Colliery NCB 1910 •Harcourts 1936 •Hardy Spicer & Co (Birfield) 1931 •Harper, Son & Bean 1917 •Philip Harris 1936 •Harris & Sheldon (Sheldonians) 1906 •Harrison (B'ham) 1925 •Harrison & Cook 1922 •Harvey Matthew 1924 •WH Haseler 1912 •OC Hawkes 1906 •Hawthorn Social 1945 •Heaton & Dugard 1923 •Hercules Cycles 1924 •Highcroft Hall 1950 •Higgs Motors 1920 •Highgate Tool & Eng 1922 •Hillmans Sports 1938 •Hills (West Bromwich) 1950 •Hill Top Foundry 1933 •Himley Pyramid 1929 •N Hingley & Sons 1919 •Hipkiss 1931 •Arthur Holden 1934 •Hollings & Guest 1917 •Holt Brewery 1921 •Henry Hope & Sons 1910 •EC Hopkins 1944 •Horseley Piggott Sports 1906 •Hoskins & Sewell 1906 •Hot Pressed Products 1936

•Howlett 1922 •Hoyland & Smith 1906 •HP Sauce 1925 •Hudson & Wright 1925 •C Hufton 1930 •Alfred Hughes & Sons 1937 •GH Hughes & Co (Big Wheel) 1932 •Hughes-Johnson Stampings 1919 •Hughes Stubbs Metal 1920 •RJ Hunt & Son 1951 •Hutton & Co. 1913 •Hyde Silas 1950 •Illston & Robson 1946 •Imperial Enamel Co 1925 •Incandescent Heat 1935 •Industrial Fan 1954 •Ingall Parsons Clive & Co 1909 •Ingram & Kemp 1919 •Thos A Ingram 1949 •Izons 1928 •James Cycle 1919 •WP James 1920 •Jarrett & Rainsford 1934 •Johnson Iron & Steel 1937 •Johnson Matthey 1944 •Jones & Percival 1920 •Jones Rims 1936 •BH Joseph 1919 •Johnsons Rolling Mills 1925 •Kalamazoo 1920 •Kean & Scott 1931 •Kegworth Works 1945 •Kemp & Sons 1936 •A Kenrick 1907 •Kenrick & Jefferson 1908 •Kingfisher 1934 •Kingsbury Colliery (NCB) 1921 •Kings Norton Metal Works 1917 •Kingston Globe (United Wire Works & Thos Haddon & Stokes) 1948 •Kingston Metal 1906 •C Kunzle 1920 •Kynoch (ICI) 1906 •Kyotts Lake Rd Depot (BCT) 1921 •Lanchester Motors 1919 •Lander St Works (GEC) 1920 •Larkins & Sons 1932 •Latch & Batchelor 1907 •W & J Lawley 1931 •Lee Howl 1928 •JB & S Lees 1935 •Thomas William Lench 1920 •Christopher Leng (Stronghold Works) 1922 •Lessor Brothers 1947 •Levi & Salaman 1906 •Levis Motors 1920 •Lewis Estates 1935 •Lightfoot Refrigeration 1935 •Light-Metal Forgings 1944 •Linread 1944 •London & North Western Rly 1908 •FH Lloyd 1926 •Richard Lloyd 1935 •London Aluminium

1919 •London Ironworks (Barlows) 1928 •Joseph Lucas (Formans Rd) 1936 •Joseph Lucas (Gt Hampton St) 1936 •Joseph Lucas (Gt King St) 1920 •Joseph Lucas (Shaftmoor Lane) 1937 •Lucas Engineering School (TID) 1937 •Richard Lunt (Lunmoor Works) 1932 •Malthouse Youth Club (Chance Bros) 1950 •WL Marrian 1932 •Marsh & Baxter (Brierley Hill) 1925 •Martindale 1912 •George Mason 1923 •H Mason 1936 •May & Padmore 1920 •A McAlpine 1920 •Wm McGeoch 1944 •McKechnie Bros 1917 •MCL & Repetition 1936 •Midland Electricity Sports Club (SNW) 1947 •MEC Sports 1947 •Midlands Electricity Sports Club (Board Headquarters) 1952 •Messengers 1911 •Metalline Enamelling 1937 •Metropolitan Cammell Carriage & Wagon 1917 •Metropolitan Cammell (Old Park Works) 1950 •Metro-Shaft (Oldbury) 1929 •Metal & Munitions 1907 •Metallic Tube Works 1907 •Microvernier 1936 •Midland Carriage & Wagon 1919 •Midland Electric Mfg 1929 •Midland Motor Cylinder 1920 •Midland Railway 1920 •Midland Red Sports 1922 •Midland Rubber 1911 •Midland Tar Distillers (Nechells) 1932 •Midland Tar Distillers (Oldbury) 1931 •Midland Tube & Forging 1917 •Midland Vinegar 1924 •H Miller 1921 •William Mills 1917 •Ministry of Pensions 1923 •Minnesota Mining & Mfg (3M Sports) formerly Durex Abrasives 1934 •The Mint (B'ham) 1906 •Mitchell & Butler 1919 •Mitre Works (J Smith) 1908 •Monitor Works 1935 •Monument Lane Loco 1920 •Moore Bros 1917 •Morgans (Tyseley) 1951 »

▲ This rusting 25 foot tall gantry, at the **Tally Ho!** ground of the **West Midlands Police** on Pershore Road, is a rare, undated example of a rig used for the training of tug-of-war.

Tug-of-war enjoyed great popularity between the two World Wars, and continued to be contested until the 1980s.

Despite having lain idle since, the rig's workings can still be seen. Concrete blocks weighing from 500 kilos to a metric tonne (representing the combined weight of a typical tug-of-war team) are attached to a steel cable, running up to a pulley at the top of the rig.

Hauling on the other end lifts the weights off the ground, no doubt adding extra muscle to the long arm of the law.

▲ Grandstand design in the lower echelons of British football rarely diverts the attention, but this 143 seat stand, which folds out from the back of a trailer, is a genuine curiosity.

Located at the **Tally Ho!** ground of the **West Midlands Police**, the stand arrived in 2005, replacing an earlier version which lasted 18 years (despite having been intended as a temporary measure).

Its presence is necessary because the league in which the police team plays requires a minimum number of covered seats, but the club is prevented by planning restrictions from building a permanent structure on the site.

Though attached to the police force's training college, the Tally Ho! ground – 'tally ho!' being the traditional cry of fox hunters on spying the fox – is effectively the southern part of what used to be a larger sports ground incorporating a polo field and the former Tally Ho! Tennis Club (*see page 116*), now a mixed-use development.

Also on the site are two adjoining bowling greens – one crown green, the other flat. This juxtaposition is one of only two known in Britain, the other being located just a few hundred yards away on Priory Road (*see page 111*).

» •Morris Commercial Cars 1924 •Morris & Jacobs 1937 •Morris Pressings 1944 •Wm Morris 1928 •Moss Gear 1925 •Motor Components 1927 •Motor Engineering 1920 •Frederick Mountford 1936 •Mulliners (Cherrywood Rd) 1931 •Mulliners (Bordesley Green) 1954 •Muntz Metal 1907 •Nathan & Hayes 1913 •National Projectile Factory 1917 •National Union of Railwaymen 1919 •Neal & Sons 1920 •Nettlefolds (Darlaston) 1921 •Guest Keen & Nettlefords (Midlands) 1907 •Nettlefolds (Kings Norton) 1906 •Newey Bros 1934 •New Hudson Cycles 1906 •New Imperial Motors 1933 •William Newman 1907 •LH Newton 1936 •Nortons (Tividale) 1947 •Oldbury Carriage Works 1919 •Oriental Tube 1931 •F & C Osler 1929 •Owen & Sons 1912 •Oyez United (Solicitors Law Stationery Society) 1951 •Palethorpes 1922 •AF Parkes 1927 •Parkinson Stove (Parkinson Monitor) 1925 •Park Mills (AW Wills & Sons) 1906 •Parker Winder & Achurch (Parwinac) 1936 •Payne & Griffiths 1937 •EJ & J Pearson (Stourbridge) 1946 •Pearson Page & Jewsbury 1937 •Peerless Stampings 1946 •Perfecta Tube Works 1911 •Permoglaze Paint 1955 •Permanent Way Dept 1929 •Perry Barr Metals 1931 •Perry's Pens 1910 •Perry Chain (Tyseley) 1908 •Peyton Hoyland & Barber 1920 •Peyton & Pepper 1923 •JA Phillips & Co (Credenda) 1906 •Phoenix Works 1906 •Phosphor Bronze (Birfield) 1913 •Pickfords 1937 •T Piggotts 1906 •Pitney Rolling Mills 1919 •Player & Mitchell 1909 •Pooleys Scale Works 1913 •Post Office Staff

1912 •Post Office Stores 1919 •Post Office Testing 1932 •Powell & Hamner (Lucas, Chester St) 1911 •FA Power 1938 •Precision Works (FE Baker) 1912 •Premier Aluminium Casting 1938 •Premier Electric (Hotpoint) 1936 •Prestage 1938 •Prometheus 1906 •Public Lighting Dept 1925 •Public Works Dept 1931 •CH Pugh 1913 •John Rabone 1908 •Ransomes 1919 •Ratcliff & Ratcliff (Gt Bridge) 1925 •Rowlands Electrical Accessories Ltd 1945 •Regal Works 1933 •Revo Electric Sports 1926 •Reynolds Rolling Mills 1947 •Reynolds Tube 1926 •Richards (Folders) 1937 •F Rippingiles 1929 •Robbins & Bradley 1938 •Alfred Roberts 1920 •Rollason Wire 1944 •Rotax 1920 •Round Oak Steelworks 1920 •Rover MOS (Acocks Green) 1949 •Rover (Solihull) 1937 •Rover Social (Tyseley) 1921 •C Rowley 1920 •Richard Thomas & Baldwin (Midlands) 1955 •CJ Rudder 1929 •Rudge Littley 1919 •Rudge Whitworth 1907 •Russell Alliance 1923 •J Russell 1936 •Geo Salter 1927 •Saltley Loco 1913 •Salisbury Transmission (Birfield) 1951 •Sanbra Sports 1933 •Thos Sanders 1925 •Sandwell Foundry 1937 •Sandwell Park Colliery 1924 •Sankey 1935 •Santoy Works 1906 •T Saveker 1945 •Savery 1925 •A Schrader 1948 •Scribbans 1934 •A Scrivener 1944 •Serck Radiators 1919 •Setton & Durward 1921 •Sharow 1954 •Sheffields 1906 •RT Shelley 1928 •Sherbourne Works 1920 •Shipway, George 1946 •Showells (Stirchley) 1911 •HC Siddons 1937 •J & J Siddons 1933 •Silk & Terry 1909 •Simplex Conduits (Creda) 1907 •Simplex Electric (Broadwell) 1948 •FR Simpson

1935 •Singer Motors 1928 •Siviter Smith 1935 •Skefco Ballbearings 1929 •Smethwick Carriage Works (B'ham Carriage) 1919 •Smethwick Drop Forgings 1950 •Smethwick Gas Dept 1933 •EH Smith 1936 •JE Smith 1930 •Smith Bros (Quinton) 1953 •Smith & Davis 1937 •Smith's Foresight 1924 •James Smith 1920 •Thos Smith (Saltley) 1907 •S Smith 1921 •Smith, Stone & Knight 1933 •Somers, Walter (Haywood Forge) 1919 •Southall & Smith 1929 •Southerton 1907 •South Staffs Waterworks 1928 •SPD Sports 1936 •Speedwell Gear Case 1948 •Sperryn 1913 •Spicer 1906 •D & L Spiers 1906 •Stampings Alliance 1936 •Standard Gas Fitting (Beau Mount) 1925 •Staybrite Works 1935 •Steel Conduits 1932 •Stewarts & Lloyds (Coombs Wood) 1907 •Streetly Works 1936 •St Stephens Works 1912 •AC Stuarts (Wordsley) 1928 •Styles Developments 1945 •SU Carburetter 1935 •Sun Cycles 1907 •Super Oil Seals 1950 •Sutherland Meter 1912 •Swallow Raincoats 1932 •Swansea Works (Bulpitt) 1912 •SWS Electric 1936 •Synyer & Beddows 1912 •Talboys Sports 1925 •Tangyes Recreation 1907 •Tansad Folders 1936 •Chas Taylor 1920 •Taylor & Challen 1917 •D & F Taylor 1909 •Taylor & Farley 1936 •Taylor Law 1910 •TB Wellings 1938 •H Terry (Redditch) 1917 •Thomas 1920 •J Thompson (Dudley) 1920 •FH Tinley 1931 •Tomeys Eureka 1919 •Townson & Coxon 1925 •Triplex Safety Glass 1931 •Triplex Foundry 1929 •Tubes Ltd Aston 1909 •Tube Investments, Day Continuation School 1950 •Tube Investments, Dept of Development & Research 1949 •Tube Products (Oldbury)

1929 •Geo Tucker Eyelet 1908 •Turner Bros (B'ham) 1937 •Turner & Simpson 1925 •Twigg 1930 •Tyseley Loco 1921 •Tyseley Metal Works 1922 •Uddeholm 1955 •Unilaw (Lawrence Cabinet) 1950 •Unity Cycle 1949 •Valor 1924 •Vaughton Works 1906 •Velocette Motor Cycles 1935 •Veritas Efisca 1933 •Veritys 1906 •Verus Works 1907 •Vickers (Weaman St) 1917 •Victoria Works 1917 •HH Vivien 1920 •Vono Sports 1933 •Chas Wade 1931 •Wales 1913 •Thos Walker 1934 •Walsall Conduits 1945 •Walsall LMS 1924 •Ward & Sons 1912 •S Ward 1925 •HW Ward 1917 •Warne Wright & Rowland 1948 •Warrilow 1922 •Warriner & Mason 1933 •Wasdell Rim 1920 •Weathershields 1938 •Webb's Sports 1931 •Webley & Scott 1925 •Wellington Tube Works 1926 •West Bromwich Spring 1948 •West Bromwich Corporation Transport 1955 •WG Allen & Sons (Tipton) 1936 •Wheway Optical 1925 •Whitfields Bedsteads 1907 •White & Pike 1906 •Whittaker Ellis 1932 •WJ Whittall 1954 •Henry Wiggin 1906 •MB Wild 1928 •Wilkes & Mapplebeck 1906 •J Wilkinson 1924 •Williams & Piggott 1922 •Clifford Williams 1955 •Edward Williams 1938 •J Williamson 1907 •Wilmot Breeden (B'ham) 1931 •Wilmot Breeden (Tyseley) 1945 •Winfield Rolling Mills 1925 •Chas Winn 1929 •S Withers 1931 •Woden Works (Steel Nut & Joseph Hampton) 1935 •Wolseley Athletic 1906 •Wolseley Sheep Shearing 1906 •Wright, Bindley & Gell 1906 •John Wright 1907 •Wrights Ropes 1919 •Wright Saddle Co 1948 •EJ Wrigley 1919 •Yate 1949 •John Yates 1923

▲ Opened in 1930, the now independently-owned six acre **Portland Road Pavilions Sports and Social Club** was, until 2003, owned by Mitchell and Butler, whose Cape Hill brewery lay to the immediate north.

(The ground should not be confused with the original Portland Road cricket and athletic grounds set up in 1869 by the Birmingham Athletic Club, located where George Dixon School now stands, on the opposite corner of Portland Road and City Road. Nor is it the same as the brewery's earlier ground, later covered by brewery expansion alongside Shenstone Road.)

In its heyday (*as seen top left in the 1950s*) Portland Road staged First Class and Second XI cricket matches for Warwickshire.

The pavilion (*above left*), similar to several other works pavilions of the period, dates from the 1930s, but suffers from the addition of a 1970s function room and balcony on the pitch-side elevation, and from awkward 1960s extensions on the bowling green side.

Elsewhere in the grounds is a small cover for spectators and patches of terracing, behind which stands the home of Warley Boxing Club, two disused tennis courts and a foreboding squash court.

Rather more inviting is the bowls pavilion (*above right*) and, on the Cape Hill boundary of the cricket pitch, a fetchingly dilapidated wooden pavilion (*top right*) thought to be the original from 1930.

That Portland Road has survived at all is a testament to its current owners. It is therefore to be hoped they will be supported by the residents of 1,400 new homes built on the brewery site.

▲ One of the few works grounds in Birmingham to remain in company ownership is the grandly titled **Transport Stadium**, Wheelers Lane, King's Heath. Originally purchased in 1908 by the Birmingham Corporation Tramways Athletic & Thrift Society – or 'The Trams' as their football team was nicknamed – the ground is run today by the West Midlands Travel (Birmingham) Sports and Social Society. The pavilions and small 1920s stand seen here in 1955 have since been replaced by a single modern pavilion of no aesthetic note.

Maintaining a sports ground was a major expense for any company, yet such were the standards that, before the 1970s, Birmingham's three professional football clubs often hired works grounds for training rather than maintain their own. Birmingham City were regulars at the Transport Stadium during the 1950s, while Villa used the Erdington grounds of Delta Metal and HP Sauce.

Indeed the Delta ground was also used as a training facility by the Spanish team playing at Villa Park during the 1966 World Cup, while Argentina based themselves at the police ground on Pershore Road.

Works football itself was a serious affair. Former professionals were signed to play or coach, with perhaps light duties offered elsewhere in the company set-up.

Larger firms such as Ansells could draw gates of up to 600, while The Trams once topped 1,000. Works AFA finals, usually held at Villa Park, St Andrew's or The Hawthorns, regularly drew in excess of 5,000.

The Works AFA was an ideal training ground for referees, with dozens progressing to officiate in the Football League. These included DH Asson, referee of the first Wembley Cup Final in 1923, Dennis Howell, later MP for Small Heath and Minister for Sport, and current FIFA accredited referee, Mike Read.

Birmingham's works teams were also watched closely by scouts from the professional game (there were complaints of poaching as early as 1910). At least 80 former works players are known to have turned professional as a result, perhaps the best known being Ron Atkinson (later manager of West Bromwich, Villa and Manchester United), who started his career with BSA Tools.

The BSA ground on Golden Hillock Road, now The Ackers Outdoor Activity Centre, is one of at least 21 works grounds still in sporting use. Others include the former Joseph Lucas ground on Moor Lane (now owned by the University of Central England), the Triplex Sports Ground (Kings Norton), the Gas Ground (Woodacre Lane), the Co-op ground (Barrows Lane), the Jaguar ground (Chester Road), the Land Rover ground (Billsmore Green), the Fujitsu ground (Sheldon) and of course the Cadbury grounds at Bournville (*see Chapter Three*).

Following a fire in 1947 which destroyed their premises at Oxhill Road, Handsworth (and sadly their archives too), the Birmingham and District Works AFA eventually raised £6,500 by public appeal to purchase new headquarters at 1081–3 Stratford Road, Hall Green (*above*), in 1957. The building remained the Works AFA's home until it was sold as a cost-cutting measure in 1983. Football in the city today is governed by the Birmingham County Football Association, formed by ten clubs in 1875. Now with over 2,400 members, the County FA is based at the Walter Goodman Stadium, Great Barr, formerly the ground of Alcan Industries.

Chapter Nine

Clubs and Pavilions

The character of a golf club can be readily discerned from its clubhouse. In scale and tone, this brick entrance to Harborne Golf Club on Tennal Road, dating from 1905, is a clear echo of solid bourgeois Harborne villas from the same period. Formed in 1893, Harborne Golf Club is one of 19 courses within Birmingham's boundaries. In 1923 its eastern edges were sold to the Corporation in order to form the nine hole Harborne Church Farm Municipal golf course.

If stadiums enjoy the highest profile in sport's architectural hierarchy, it is in the club pavilion that we find the beating heart of grassroots sport.

The Birmingham area has an estimated 1,100 sports clubs, including some 200 for cricket, 154 for bowls, 50 for rugby, 46 for tennis, plus dozens of others for hockey, athletics, badminton, squash, swimming, darts, angling and sundry other sports.

For those clubs able to own or rent their own facilities, the pavilion, or clubhouse, is the core of their being, a building whose functions transcend sport. For regulars it offers sanctuary from the home and workplace. For the committee it is the club's main source of revenue, and often the main drain on resources too, when roofs leak or pipes burst.

Pavilions and clubhouses differ considerably in scale and substance. Golf clubhouses often attempt to emulate the suburban villas in whose midst they are located. They have substantial dining rooms and function suites. Bowls and tennis club pavilions

are, conversely, often hardly more than overgrown sheds (but are loved equally for that very quality).

Where architectural details are to be found, these tend towards the homely vernacular style favoured by generations of club officials since the Victorian period (in Birmingham as throughout

Britain). But as this chapter shows, where funds have been available – at private educational establishments for example – designers have delivered modern pavilions of considerable verve.

One of the enduring delights of Birmingham's sportscape is how many clubs and pavilions

Moseley Ashfield Cricket Club's timber scoreboard has weathered well since its inauguration in 1937. Ashfield's charming ground, between Yardley Wood Road and Moseley Golf Course, opened in 1904. Its pavilion features ornate leaded windows. The ground also features Moseley Football Club's 1914–18 granite war memorial, formerly located at The Reddings.

lie hidden from public view, behind hedges or fences, down tracks between houses. It is not uncommon for even neighbours to be ignorant of their presence.

Yet the activities organised within help cement communities, provide continuity, promote fitness and, just as importantly – whether one cares or not about sport – offer a bulwark against development. Sports clubs are unofficial guardians of great swathes of our urban green space.

Most club activists work hard without reward. But in doing so they face increasing levels of bureaucracy and costs. For while they can now claim tax relief if they register as Community Amateur Sports Clubs – of which there were approximately 3,500 nationwide in early 2006, out of a possible total of 110,000 clubs – they also face much higher charges under the Licensing Act 2003.

Clubs with buildings of historic value face additional problems.

Sports governing bodies tend to grant aid larger clubs who, in the case of tennis, for example, can provide floodlights, which is not always possible in built-up residential areas.

Meanwhile funding from such agencies as the National Lottery and Sport England's Community Investment Fund favours the construction of new buildings in which function overrides form.

This has led to a new breed of uniform, unimaginative pavilions – the sheds of today, as it were – or to the poorly planned incremental development of existing buildings.

Birmingham suffers no more from this than anywhere else. Yet that is no excuse, given the vital role that grassroots clubs play in enhancing and stabilising the historic and natural environment.

▲ Bowls and tennis clubs proved ideal for slotting into the grid of late 19th and early 20th century suburban planning. They were the right size, needed only one access point within the block, and added value – monetary and social – to the houses whose rear gardens they backed onto.

With eight courts and a cramped pavilion, the **Moseley Tennis Club**, Billesley Lane, formed in 1923 and now with over 250 members, illustrates this symbiotic relationship.

But there are pressures too.

With a membership of around 50, three hard courts and a trim wooden pavilion dating from 1939, **Beechcroft Tennis Club** (*right*), tucked away off Stratford Road, Hall Green, occupies less than half an acre of land owned by Hall Green Parochial Council. The club has no bar, only a nine year lease, and little chance of outside funding.

The Lawn Tennis Association, for example, prefers to fund larger clubs with more coaching facilities and the option of floodlights. Thus Beechcroft must organise regular fundraising events, while sharing out maintenance duties amongst the club's handier members.

▲ When the fish pond in front of the clubhouse at **Handsworth Golf Club** was drained shortly before this photograph was taken in 1965, hundreds of golf balls were dredged up, including many an old 'gutty' (or gutta percha ball) from the early 20th century.

Accessed from Sunningdale Close (named after one of Britain's most prominent courses), the Handsworth clubhouse has at its core the original pavilion, dating from 1906, which, in common with the headquarters of most golf clubs, has undergone considerable expansion during its lifetime.

The Handsworth and West Bromwich border areas are rich in golfing facilities. The Hill Top Municipal Course – opened in 1979 in response to local demand – adjoins the western edge of Handsworth's, while to the south west, immediately beyond Handsworth Cemetery, lies Sandwell Park Golf Course, with its impressive modern clubhouse. To the north west is the nine hole Dartmouth Golf Course, while there are pitch and putt facilities at both Sandwell Valley Country Park and Sandwell Recreation Ground.

◀ Barely distinguishable from a family home, the clubhouse of **Moseley Golf Club**, Springfield Road, was originally a 19th century building called Billesley Hall Farm (which was itself built on the site of a medieval house, Bulley Hall).

The golf club – the oldest in the city of Birmingham – took over the estate when it formed in 1892, but erected its own pavilion (a standard Boulton and Paul prefabricated clubhouse), in 1897. It then moved into Billesley Hall Farm in 1914, before redeveloping the building as we see it today in 1924.

Today the club owns a total of 120 acres, including the adjoining ground of Moseley Ashfield Cricket Club, on Yardley Wood Road, north of Coldbath Pool.

A contrasting style of clubhouse, with no pretence of domestic familiarity, is that of the **Robin Hood Golf Club** (*left*), on St Bernard's Road, Solihull.

Costing £90,000 and opened in 1966, it was designed by David Charles Architects and in both scale and form indicates the trend followed by many golf clubs in the post war era towards greater provision for social and catering facilities. The clubhouse's opening also marked the completion of the golf course's realignment, in which 10 acres of the club's old course were sold off for housing and a further 26 acres purchased.

▶ Birmingham-born architect John Madin is revered and reviled in almost equal measure for his role in the redevelopment of Birmingham city centre during the 1960s and 1970s. Among his landmark commissions were the Central Library, Post and Mail Building and National Westminster House.

But one of Madin's earliest designs was this 1950s American ranch-style clubhouse at the **Shirley Golf Club**, Stratford Road, Monkspath. The building was commissioned by the Birmingham Jewish Golf Society, who had set up their own course – on the site of the recently closed Shirley Park racecourse (*see page 120*) – in response to discrimination against Jewish people wishing to take up the game.

Opened in July 1959, the *Birmingham Sketch* noted that 'devotees of the modern school will find a great source of satisfaction in the manner in which the architect has provided a building beautiful in design and position, at the same time offering every possible facility to the members of the Club'.

As with much of Madin's best work, the clean lines of the Shirley clubhouse make a powerful impression, as do those of the more linear pavilion at King Edward's School, Eastern Road (*right*). Built in 1965 at a cost of £38,500, it was designed by JL Osborne.

◀ Designed by Michael Edwards Associates of Harborne and opened in August 2004 at a cost of £1.5m, the **Alan Lee Pavilion** at **Solihull School** is an excellent example of contemporary pavilion design.

A light and airy building utilising a blend of brick and timber facings with a metallic curved roof, the building acts as the centrepiece of the school's abundant 53 acre playing fields. In addition to changing rooms, a treatment room, conference room and coffee bar, the pavilion also houses the shirt worn at the 2003 Rugby World Cup Final by England captain and Silhillian, Martin Johnson.

Also in the education sector is the pavilion at the **University of Central England's Moor Lane Playing Fields** site (*below left*) formerly the works ground of Joseph Lucas (*see Chapter Eight*).

Opened in 2003 and designed by Robothams Architects, the £4.5m pavilion features 22 changing rooms serving the centre's 13 sports pitches, alongside conference and banqueting facilities catering for up to 500 guests and a large first floor terrace.

Unashamedly modern in both style and use of materials, this ambitious project is a worthy successor to the likes of Rowheath Pavilion (*see Chapter Three*) in that sport is but one of its core functions.

Chapter Ten

Parks and Pools

A 21st century blend of roller rink, adventure playground and cycle track, the King's Norton Wheeled Sports Park, opened in 2005, is one of a new generation of facilities utilising moulded concrete and a power-floated concrete floor. Designed by Planet Skate in consultation with Laid Back Leisure, local skateboarders and BMX bikers, its ten sculptured elements include a split level half-pipe, spine ramp and grind box.

Our fourth thematic study concerns the 'green' and 'blue' areas on the map, that is, Birmingham's publicly accessible open spaces and waterscapes, where so much of the city's grassroots sporting activity occurs.

Such spaces are more numerous than even many Brummies might imagine, and more than enough to challenge negative perceptions held by critics unfamiliar with the city's topography.

According to Birmingham City Council there are 470 parks, recreation grounds and public open spaces within the city boundaries, covering a total area of 7,900 acres (3,200 hectares), a figure believed to be unmatched by any other British city.

And as the map on page 95 illustrates, for an inland city Birmingham has a significant number of lakes, ponds, rivers, streams and canals, adding a surprising dimension to the city's recreational life.

Turning first to the green spaces, Birmingham's earliest parks were privately owned. They included Bridgman's Gardens in

An early 20th century hexagonal pay booth serves the Crazy Golf green at Cannon Hill Park, Edgbaston. One of three city parks to have won the Civic Trust's coveted Green Flag award, Cannon Hill also has tennis courts, bowling greens and a boating lake. Its former open air swimming pool is shown on page 29.

Aston (where Birmingham's first cricket match took place in 1751), Spring Gardens in Deritend, with its woods, grottoes and arbour, Moseley Street's elegant Apollo Hotel grounds, and the exclusive Botanical Gardens in Edgbaston, opened in 1832.

From 1892–1914 there were also botanical gardens on Wake Green Road, Moseley (in the grounds of what is now Moseley School).

But perhaps the best known of Birmingham's early private parks lay in the grounds of Duddeston Hall, former home of the Holte family, 'four furlongs east of Birmingham'. After the death of the last incumbent in 1738 the hall was turned into a travellers' hotel, with a cockpit first advertised there in 1746.

As the site developed it was renamed Vauxhall Gardens (after the larger and more established

pleasure grounds in London of that era), its proprietor's aim being to provide 'genteeler sort of people' with concerts, dancing, firework displays and balloon ascents. There were also the usual grottoes, a bowling green and a billiard room.

In common with its London counterpart – and numerous similar establishments around Britain – Vauxhall Gardens eventually became notorious for its bawdier clientele. As a result, by the 1830s, with Birmingham's industrial sprawl encroaching and the city's first railway station opened on its borders, Vauxhall fell into neglect and in 1850 was built over. (It lay on what it is now the east side of Vauxhall Road, by Duddeston station.)

If private enterprise alone could not be depended upon to deliver recreational space for the city's

CRAZY GOLF
TICKETS ➡

growing population, the issue was next taken up by politicians and philanthropists.

In 1833 a Parliamentary Select Committee on Public Walks highlighted the need for action, a process which led to the opening of the first public parks in Preston (1833), Manchester (1846) and Birkenhead (1847).

Birmingham was rather slower to follow suit, and even then it was largely as a result of private benefaction that the city's first public park opened in August 1856. This was Adderley Park, Saltley, laid out on ten acres of land donated by CB Adderley (later Lord Norton), at a peppercorn rent of 5s per annum.

Calthorpe Park followed nine months later, using 31 acres donated by Lord Calthorpe (*see Chapter Two*). Included in the design was provision for cricket, rounders, trap-ball, battledore, quoits, gymnastics and archery.

In 1858 a third park opened, this time with Queen Victoria performing the honours. Aston Hall and Park was initially run by a private company, albeit one with a philanthropic outlook, after the Corporation baulked at the £35,000 required to purchase the land. But when the company subsequently struggled, a lower purchase price of £19,000 was agreed for part of the site, allowing it to be opened to the public as a 'free hall and park forever'.

(Across the road from Aston Park lay the Aston Lower Grounds, a commercially run pleasure ground – *see Chapter Four* – which may be considered a true successor to Vauxhall Gardens.)

Birmingham's three public parks now totalled 91 acres, which for a population of 300,000 was still relatively inadequate. Yet it

would require another gift in order for a fourth park to be created, in Edgbaston in 1873.

Destined to become the city's pride and joy, and host to a myriad of events and entertainments to the present day, Cannon Hill Fields were gifted by a wealthy landowner, Miss Louisa Anne Ryland, on condition that the resultant park would not, as had Adderley and Calthorpe Parks, be named after her. Moreover, she also paid for the construction of a pavilion, two boating lakes, a boat house and a bathing pool.

Two further parks, Highgate Park and Summerfield Park, opened at public expense in 1876. This was followed in 1906 by the formation of the Birmingham Playgrounds and Open Spaces Association, whose leading lights – Joseph Chamberlain, George Cadbury, William Kendrick and

John Sutton Nettlefold – did much to highlight the need for even more recreational space. During its 18 month lifespan (before turning its attention to housing developments), the Association was responsible for securing eight further public open spaces, totalling nearly 30 acres. These included Garrison Lane Recreation Ground, Bordesley, laid out on the site of demolished slum properties and equipped for 'gymnastics', or what we would now call a children's playground.

To these were added, by 1914, three further parks: Victoria (later Small Heath) Park – another gift from Miss Ryland – Handsworth Park, and Queens Park, Harborne.

After decidedly slow beginnings therefore, the development of Birmingham's parks finally caught up with the comparatively plentiful provision of public baths, »

Football in Birmingham's oldest municipal park, Adderley Park, which lies just east of the site of the former Vauxhall Gardens and the city's first railway station at Duddeston. In the distance is Birmingham's 'mini-Manhattan' skyline, with Selfridges and the Rotunda to the left and the Post Office Tower to the right. Few of the park's trees survived the tornado which devastated parts of the city in July 2005.

▶ This rustic boathouse, erected in 1958, adorns the pool of **Moseley Private Park**. The 11 acre park, whose layout is thought to have been influenced by Humphry Repton in the late 18th century (an ice house from that period still survives), originally formed the northern edge of the Moseley Hall estate and was saved from development by local residents in 1899, when Salisbury Road dissected the estate.

Ever since, remarkably and, it would seem, uniquely in urban Britain, the park has belonged entirely to its keyholders, who currently pay £33 per year for the privilege and, in so doing, become shareholders in the Moseley Park and Pool Company. Apart from occasional open days subscriptions are the park's only income.

Based in the park are an angling club and the Chantry Tennis Club, one of whose courts was formerly a bowling green.

Another boathouse is that of the **Bournville Model Yacht and Power Boat Club** (*right*), based at Valley Parkway, Woodbrooke Road. The adjoining lake was created in 1932 as part of the Unemployment Relief Scheme, and originally had its own boat repair shop, along with a model railway and flag station. Racing is still held twice weekly and the club attracts enthusiasts from Europe and North America.

» swimming pools, laundries and libraries (*see Chapter Seventeen*), reflecting the city's rising status as a beacon of municipal activity.

There remained notable gaps nevertheless. In 1923, for example, 770 boys were charged before magistrates with playing football in the streets, an indication that open space in the inner city areas was still severely restricted.

To ensure that this imbalance was not replicated in the expanding outer suburbs the Corporation had to adopt a much broader strategic approach to leisure provision, beyond the network of public parks.

Thus the inter-war period saw the local authority become a direct provider of sports facilities.

Though the inner-outer city imbalance continued, by the late 1940s the Corportation had extended its remit to around 400 tennis courts, 150 football pitches and dozens of bowling greens. It also provided facilities for many of the city's 291 cricket teams, along with pitches for rugby and hockey, and even a few greens for pitch and putt. This was a golden era in Birmingham's parks provision. Every sizeable park had its park keeper. Maintenance levels were high. Boats and boathouses were plentiful, and the city's bandstands reverberated to the sound of music most summer evenings and weekends.

The use of parks as centres of public entertainment had assumed particular importance during the Second World War, when, in order to boost morale, and to provide diversions during the summer months, the government encouraged all local authorities to organise public entertainments.

Thus, in 1942, was born the *Brighter Birmingham Campaign*, with a variety of free events, held mostly in the city's parks.

Indeed, so extensive did these activities become that in the late 1940s the Corporation produced weekly guides, detailing all the concerts, plays, dances, exhibitions, carnivals and fetes, fairgrounds and circuses. Cannon Hill staged an annual tulip festival, while November meant fireworks displays at several parks.

In 1954 the city's first *Festival of Entertainments* was launched, aimed at providing mass entertainment without cultural pretensions.

Such events continued through the 1950s, but as losses mounted in the following decade, gradually they became confined to just a few parks, with Cannon Hill Park regarded as the flagship.

Mirroring this decline in park events was a wider move away from traditional sports to more participation in minority games, such as table tennis, volleyball, basketball and badminton, all of which were better played indoors, at multi-purpose halls attached to schools, churches and community centres. (Birmingham's first such facility was the Munrow Sports Centre at Birmingham University, opened in 1966.) Confirming this trend was the 1960 Wolfenden Report on Sport in the Community, which recommended 'large barns' be erected to accommodate the new generation of sports.

So it was that from 1960 onwards the indoor leisure centre became the 'must have' sports facility for local authorities.

During the next three decades over 30 such centres were erected throughout the Birmingham area (for example the Small Heath Leisure Centre, Muntz Street, opened in 1975).

Though few would win any awards for aesthetics, their value both in providing vital amenities for minority sports and in addressing the shortage of facilities in the city's more economically deprived wards cannot be overstated.

But the investment required to construct, equip and maintain them did mean that traditional local authority facilities in parks and playing fields were starved of funds, setting off a long and steady cycle of decline.

Substandard pitches, dilapidated changing rooms and vandalised toilets were to become the hallmark of public sporting provision from the 1970s onwards, in Birmingham as in many other parts of urban Britain. And as facilities worsened, so too, inevitably, did participation levels fall, especially among youngsters from poorer households, for whom the cost of joining private sports clubs remained prohibitive.

The late 20th century trend was not all downwards. Certain inner city wards were to benefit from some imaginative schemes, such as the creation of a network of mini-parks on redundant land around Hay Mills and Balsall Heath. The recent development of the King's Norton Wheeled Sports Park (*see page 92*) also illustrates how sport's changing cultural landscape has been reflected in parks' provision, with more emphasis being placed on individual fitness – for example, trim trails – and on smaller Multi-Use Games Areas, or MUGAs.

All the same, traditional team sports continue to dominate the Council's future agenda.

In its draft document, *Birmingham Parks and Playing Fields Strategy*, released in January 2006,

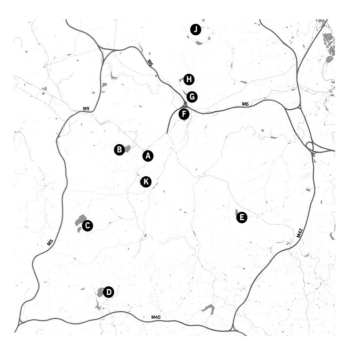

Ordnance Survey Maps © Crown Copyright. All Rights Reserved. English Heritage, 100019088, 2006

▲ The Birmingham area possesses a surprising number of water features, as this 'blue map' of the city illustrates. Although the rivers Cole, Rea and Tame are too narrow or discreet to be regarded by the public as major geographic features, water defines and identifies several areas: Sparkbrook, Bournbrook, Stechford, Moorpool and Bromford Bridge, for example.

The city sits at the apex of the national canal network, with three converging in the Brindley Place/Gas Street basin area (A). Feeding these canals required a network of reservoirs – principally those at Edgbaston (B), Bartley (C), Upper Bittell (D) and Olton (E) – while population growth necessitated the construction of further reservoirs, such as at Aston, now Salford Park (F), Lower Witton, now Brookvale Park (G), and Middle Witton, now Witton Lakes (H).

As related in earlier chapters, industrial development also led to the creation of a network of pools. Sutton Park's eight pools (J) were all formed from the 15th century onwards to serve local mills, as was the Great Pool in Edgbaston (K) in the 16th century.

Finally, numerous pools were created in Birmingham parks during the 19th and early 20th centuries, such as at Small Heath and Handsworth.

Added to a scattering of smaller natural pools and former marl pits, these water features provide a range of recreational opportunities. Pleasure boats and outdoor skating are no longer commonplace, but the Birmingham Angling Association is still Britain's largest (*see page 98*), while sailing and other watersports are popular at such reservoirs as Edgbaston, Olton Mere and Bartley Green.

▲ One of urban Britain's finest waterscapes is the **Edgbaston Reservoir**, shown here in 2005 from the west. Covering 62 acres (25 hectares), with a maximum depth of 13 metres, it was engineered by Thomas Telford from 1825–29, on the site of Rotton Park. Its purpose was, and still is, to act as a feeder to the Birmingham Canal, which runs just beyond the 336 metre long dam seen at the top.

From 1860 pleasure boats operated from the site of what until recently was the Tower Ballroom (*on the right hand end of the dam*), but which from c.1876 to the 1920s was a roller skating rink.

Nowadays there are clubs for canoeing, rowing, windsurfing and sailing, and the reservoir is also Birmingham's most popular destination for anglers.

Inevitably, its delightful walks and views, and its proximity to the city centre, make this a desirable location for waterside development. A consultation exercise was thus launched in 2005 to investigate how sensitive issues relating to its future might be managed in the years ahead.

» the Council outlined how, by 2020, Birmingham intends to provide better sports facilities, in more parts of the city, appropriate to the needs of every ability range.

In early 2006, it calculated, there was a total of 561 pitches within the city in all sectors (public, private and educational), of which 429 were hired out by over 850 teams per week; 69 per cent of them for football, 18 per cent for cricket, ten per cent for rugby and three per cent for hockey. The city also had around 100 bowling greens (*see Chapter Twelve*).

In short, traditional sports continue to dominate the local sporting scene.

Also of interest was the report's findings concerning the range of team sports played. In addition to football, cricket, rugby and hockey, the city also has teams for rounders, lacrosse and kabbadi.

At the same time the Council also published its draft strategy on the future of parks and open spaces. Almost half the city's wards, it was found, have yet to meet the target level of two hectares of public open space per 1,000 people, while only six of 39 wards satisfied the target level of 1.2 hectares of playing fields per 1,000 people.

Progress was in hand, however. Ward End Park was to receive £4 million for improvements, while in 2005–06 Handsworth Park underwent a £10 million makeover. The city could also boast a completely new park, in Newhall Valley, Sutton Coldfield.

That said, after years of under investment, the challenges facing parks provision in the future are considerable; not only in terms of sporting provision but in the conservation of great swathes of the city's historic environment.

Members of the Midland Sailing Club have no shortage of landmarks at Edgbaston Reservoir. To the east, beyond the dam (*above left*) stands the Post Office Tower (built 1963–67), while to the south east (*above*) is the Birmingham Waterworks Tower (1870), which, together with the adjacent Perrott's Folly (1758), is said to have been the inspiration for Tolkein's *The Two Towers*. (He spent part of his childhood in the vicinity.) To the south west (*left*) the spire of St Augustine's Church (1879) rises above the trees.

▲ Members of The Plumbers Arms Fishing Club – one of many such clubs affiliated to the **Birmingham Anglers Association** – pose for Albert Wilkes in 1926.

The BAA had formed in 1883 at The Old Green Man pub in Lancaster Street, primarily to lobby railway companies for reduced fares for anglers at weekends.

At its peak in the 1970s, 1,200 clubs and 68,000 individuals were affiliated to the BAA, making it the world's largest angling association. Most clubs were attached to sports or social clubs, pubs or factories. Longbridge alone had 30 angling clubs. Joseph Lucas had 15.

Despite its wider public image as a solitary and somewhat old fashioned, time-consuming pursuit, fishing continues to be hugely popular, with an estimated three million adherents nationwide. The BAA is still, moreover, Britain's largest association, with 200 clubs and 10,000 members registered in 2005. Currently it oversees fishing on 500 miles of rivers, 70 miles of canals and 15 lakes across the Midlands.

For its part, Birmingham City Council issues permits for 19 pools, including at **Ward End Park** (*above right*) and **Brookvale Park** (*right*), where there is also a sailing club.

Of course the presence of fish is, in environmental terms, a useful indicator of water quality, with roach, bream, carp and perch being most commonly fished in Birmingham waters, plus chubb and eel in canals. But recent evidence suggests that fishing itself confers social benefits as well.

Originally set up in Durham but adopted by the Bournville Village Trust in 2002, the *Get Hooked on Fishing* scheme seeks to introduce young offenders, socially disadvantaged youths and drug users to angling as a means of improving their quality of life and reducing anti-social behaviour.

In its first four years, nearly 1,500 Midlanders aged 8–17 joined the scheme, of which 90 per cent have carried on fishing, and only two per cent have reoffended. Participants have also helped to clean up and restock local waters, such as Rowheath Lake.

Fishing at dusk at Salford Park, with the elevated section of the Aston Expressway in the distance. As this image illustrates, despite the overwhelming presence of Europe's largest single road interchange – which opened in 1972 – there is a hidden and curiously beguiling network of green and wooded spaces in and around Spaghetti Junction, popular with joggers as well as anglers. One such space, to the immediate north west (*just out of view on the centre right of the aerial photograph*) is the Magnet Centre, the seven acre sports ground originally laid out during the 1920s by GEC (*see page 77*).

▲ Just as some of Birmingham's finest sports grounds are to be found hidden behind hedges or up unmarked tracks, so the city's waterscapes appear in some of the unlikeliest places – none more so than the former Aston Reservoir, now **Salford Park**, located in the shadows of the Gravelly Hill Interchange (better known as Spaghetti Junction).

For season 2005–06 a day's fishing permit from the City Council cost £2.85 (£1.50 concessions), though of course the cost of rods and equipment can run into thousands. Anglers have thus unfortunately found themselves increasingly prey to thieves, while the fish stocks themselves are said to have suffered from greater numbers of cormorants in the area.

Also seen here is the **Power League** five-a-side centre on the site of the former Salford Park cycle track (*see page 51*), while in the top left stands Villa Park and the wooded slopes of Aston Park. In the top right, beyond the Perry Barr Greyhound Stadium are the Perry Hall Playing Fields and the grounds of the University of Central England (*see Chapters Four and Eight*).

Chapter Eleven

Made in Birmingham

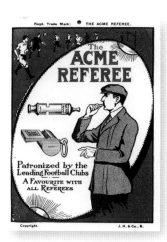

With sales of over 200 million, no Birmingham product has had a greater impact on sport than the referee's whistle, manufactured by Joseph Hudson & Co., of Hockley, since 1884, and advertised here in 1909. In particular, Hudson's Acme Thunderer has been blasted at World Cup, UEFA, Olympic and FA Cup finals, at Canadian ice hockey, NFL gridiron and championships for netball, hockey, volleyball and basketball. A blow by blow account of its origins follows on page 106.

The oft-repeated description of Birmingham as 'city of a thousand trades' was no idle boast. Many of the goods produced, moreover, were aimed at the sports market, at home and abroad, with the majority manufactured from metal – the very foundation of Birmingham's growth since the 16th century.

Most prominent among these products were cups, trophies and medals, made predominantly by three companies (Elkington's, Vaughton's and Fattorini's), and referee's whistles (by Hudson's), all based in Hockley, now better known as the Jewellery Quarter.

By 1870 some 10,000 people were employed in hundreds of workshops crammed into the area, a number that would rise rapidly by 1914. A similar concentration of craftsmen was concerned with the production of sporting guns and rifles. By 1874 329 gun makers were listed in the city, of which 210 were in the Gun Quarter, south and west of Snow Hill.

Elsewhere, in areas such as Aston, Small Heath and Tyseley, there were medium and large

companies manufacturing bicycles (such as Dunlop, Hercules, Phillips and New Hudson); motor cycles (BSA, Norton and Ariel) and components, such as chains, gears and saddles. Reuben Heaton & Sons, founded in 1857 and based in Aston, were leading makers of fishing tackle. In the 1920s the Birmingham Aluminium Casting Co starting making one of the world's first 'all-metal' tennis rackets, called the Birmal.

None of these businesses were founded on the manufacture of sporting goods alone, but the innovative approach of their designers, allied to the precision skills of the workforce – all, crucially, backed up by effective sales teams – made them ideally suited to capitalise on Britain and the empire's rapidly growing love affair with organised sport.

Nor were the 'thousand trades' confined to metal bashing.

Clapshaw & Cleave produced cricket bats and tennis rackets in Small Heath. Thomas Padmore & Sons of Edmund Street were prominent makers of billiard and snooker tables until 1940, and

there was hardly a child in pre-1970s Britain who did not, at one time or another, play with either a game or toy manufactured by the Chad Valley company of Harborne.

For adults, millions of golf and tennis balls were produced at Dunlop's in Erdington.

In common with so much of Britain's manufacturing sector, Birmingham's sports goods industry has largely been lost to South East Asia or the Indian subcontinent. The closure in early 2006 of Webley and Scott, based in Rubery, also highlighted the demise of the city's sporting firearms industry.

Indeed today, only in the Jewellery Quarter is Birmingham's manufacturing tradition maintained, so far as it relates to sports-related products.

But that does at least mean that if you are at a sports event almost anywhere in Britain, or indeed in many parts of the globe, and hear a whistle blown, or see a medal or a cup being presented, the chances are that the item will have been, as it was a century ago, 'Made in Birmingham'.

▲ Bon viveur, fox hunter and Arsenal director Hugh Cecil Lowther, the 5th Earl of Lonsdale (1857–1944), gave his name to a size of cigar, a range of sportswear and to the decorative gold and porcelain belts that, since 1911, have been awarded to British boxing champions. (The first winner was 'Bombardier' Billy Wells, otherwise noted as the banger of the gong for Rank films.)

This modern Lonsdale Belt, made from sterling silver with 24 carat gold plating, and with Lonsdale's portrait hand painted in powdered glass, was manufactured by **Thomas Fattorini Ltd** of Hockley.

Fattorini's have been making Lonsdale Belts since 1988, but have supplied the sporting world with badges, medals, cups and trophies for considerably longer, having originally been founded as a Skipton jewellery shop by an Italian immigrant in 1827.

Fattorini's Bradford branch also designed the current FA Cup, which was made in Sheffield and first awarded in 1911, after the previous version, made by the Birmingham firm of Vaughton's, was withdrawn by the Football Association (*see next page*).

Fattorini's first Birmingham works were established in 1919 in Hockley Street, the company moving to its present site (by architects Mansell and Mansell, 1894–95), on the corner of Regent Street and Frederick Street (*right*) in 1927.

Following the closure of the company's last remaining Yorkshire outlets the Birmingham office now retains the original pencil drawings for the FA Cup.

Other Fattorini products include FA Cup winners' medals, blazer buttons for golf's Royal and Ancient Club, along with various items for football's leading international federations, as well as the Premier League, the International Olympic Committee and the Lawn Tennis Association. However, the majority of their 25,000 accounts are with grassroots clubs and associations.

The company, which employs over 100 staff, remains in family hands, with three brothers now representing the sixth generation of Fattorini's at management level.

▶ On the corner of Newhall Street and Charlotte Street (adjacent to the Birmingham Assay Office), the showroom of **Elkington & Co**, as shown here in an early 20th century brochure, was an Aladdin's Cave of cups, trophies, plates, shields, badges and medallions.

Elkington's, part of whose works were later converted into the Science Museum, were pioneers of electro-plating, a process patented c.1840. Perhaps their most illustrious product in the world of sport is the silver salver that has been presented to the winner of the Wimbledon Ladies Singles title since 1886. Often referred to as the 'Rosewater Dish', the salver is 48 cm in diameter and was crafted in 1864, at a cost of 50 guineas.

In competition with Elkington's was **P Vaughton & Sons** of Great Hampton Street. That one of the sons was Howard Vaughton, who played for Aston Villa and England during the period 1880–87, no doubt helped when, in 1888, the newly formed Football League was looking for its first Championship trophy and medals.

Vaughton's gained a further commission in 1895, from the Football Association, after the original FA Cup – first awarded in 1873 – was stolen from the window of William Shillcock's sports goods shop in Newtown Row, having just been won by Aston Villa. The FA fined the club £25 for their carelessness, but as Villa had already insured the 'Little Tin Idol' for £200 (at the insistence of the FA), a replica was easily afforded.

As it transpired, Vaughton's new trophy had to be replaced just 16 years later, in 1911, because Manchester United made several copies of it, thereby breaching the FA's copyright. As mentioned on the previous page, the third, and current FA Cup trophy was then supplied by the Bradford branch of Fattorini's. Vaughton's 1895 replica was, meanwhile, donated to the FA President, Lord Kinnaird.

For the next three years the Football League placed their medal contract with Fattorini's of Bradford too, until complaints from Blackburn and Notts County about the quality of their winners' medals in 1914 saw Vaughton's back in favour. They have supplied the League ever since.

Vaughton's is now owned by WH Darby of Well Street, but their splendid former Gothic Works (*below right*), built in 1902 to the designs of Sidney H Vaughton, and vacated in 1999, can still be seen on Livery Street.

As to Vaughton's 1895 FA Cup trophy, in May 2005 it was bought at a Christie's auction for £420,000, by David Gold, chairman of Birmingham City.

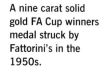

A nine carat solid gold FA Cup winners medal struck by Fattorini's in the 1950s.

▲ An unidentified motorcycle club gathers at a petrol station on the corner of Summer Hill Road and Powell Street c.1927–28.

Birmingham manufacturers dominated the British motorbike industry, with an estimated 100 companies involved in production at one time or another. Four of these would figure prominently in competitive action.

Norton, established in 1898, won its first Isle of Man TT race in 1907, before setting up a factory in Bracebridge Street, Aston, in 1916. Velocette (founded in 1905) found similar success shortly after moving from Aston to York Road,

Hall Green, in 1926, while Ariel motorcycles, established on Dale Road, Selly Oak, in 1897, were less successful on the road but performed well in scrambling in the 1950s and developed a keen following for their stylish designs.

But most successful of all was the Birmingham Small Arms company. Founded in 1861 as a conglomeration of 16 local gunmakers, BSA started motorcycle production in 1911 and by the 1920s had become the world's leading manufacturer, employing over 13,000 workers at their 25 acre factory on Armoury Road, Small Heath.

In the late 1930s BSA launched the acclaimed 500cc Gold Star racing bike and, in 1954, took five of the first six places at the gruelling Daytona 200 in Florida.

Despite further track success over the next two decades, like most British bike makers, BSA fell prey to poor management and competition from Japan.

Norton vacated Aston in 1962. A year later Ariel ceased production in Selly Oak. Velocette closed in 1971 and in 1973 the BSA works were finally shut down.

From 100 to zero, Birmingham's motorcycle industry lasted barely 75 years.

▲ As a means of research and development, as a marketing tool, and for the sheer hell of it, manufacturers and designers of bicycles, motorcycles and motor cars have, from the very start, competed with each other on the race track. But few cycle makers went to the lengths of **Dunlop**.

Shown here at London's Crystal Palace in 1897 are members of the formidable Dunlop Tyre Quint Pacing Team.

The role of a company's pacing team is to set a fast pace ahead of the actual racing cyclists (a task undertaken today by motorbikes or cars). Such pacing teams might consist of two, three, four or, as here, five seater bikes.

Based at the Para Mills in Aston Cross since 1891, the Dunlop company had been founded in Dublin two years earlier. Its origins are the stuff of legend. In 1888, John Boyd Dunlop, a Scottish vet

living in Belfast, had noted how his son's tricycle, fitted with the usual solid rubber tyres of the day, vibrated uncomfortably on rough terrain. To counter this effect Dunlop encased the wheels in thin rubber sheets, glued together and inflated with a foot pump.

Realising the commercial potential of his work – a similar concept had been tried, though not perfected, by another Scotsman in 1845 – Dunlop went into production, thus transforming the entire notion of wheeled transport.

To secure supplies, in 1898 it bought a Birmingham India Rubber company, Byrne Brothers. It also purchased plantations in Malaya and Ceylon, before establishing a factory in Kobe, Japan, in 1909.

Above all, by using a Doughty Press, Dunlop managed to reduce the time needed to mould and vulcanize each tyre from two hours to three minutes.

Establishing a virtual monopoly of the British tyre market, the firm's status was further enhanced in 1916 when it purchased 260 acres of farmland in Erdington and built the vast Fort Dunlop works, soon to be dominated by the iconic Base Stores, the building which, to many, *is* Fort Dunlop.

Although bicycle manufacture ceased in 1914, Dunlop car tyres were used in successful world land speed record attempts in 1938 and 1947, while during the 1950s the firm notched an unrivalled 66 Grand Prix victories.

With over three million square feet of factory space, five miles of marshalling yards, research facilities, training schools and extensive sports grounds for its 10,000 employees, Fort Dunlop formed the hub of a world empire stretching across 54 countries.

Since 1999 the company has been part of the giant Goodyear

Corporation of America, and although it retains a factory on the Erdington site, producing tyres for the motorsport industry, the Base Stores building is being converted into a hotel and apartments.

But the Dunlop name lives on elsewhere in the sports world. In 1959 the company took over its rival tennis manufacturer Slazenger, while it also produces golf equipment and sportswear, though predominantly in the Far East rather than Birmingham.

◀ Dignitaries gather at Rocky Lane, Aston, in November 1933, to watch the three millionth **Hercules** bicycle come off the company's production line. Watching intently is Sir Macolm Campbell (*far left*), who nine months earlier had established a world land speed record of 272.46 mph at Daytona and was now attempting to enter political life as a Conservative MP.

Although the manufacture of bicycles originated in Coventry – spurred by the invention of the first Rover 'safety bicycle' in 1885 (that is, the model on which today's bicycles are based) – by 1914 Birmingham companies dominated the industry, employing almost 10,000 workers in total.

At the time of this photocall, Hercules alone employed 4,000, making it the world's largest bicycle factory. Close behind them were BSA (based on Armoury Road, Small Heath) and the Nottingham firm Raleigh. Other Birmingham bicycle makers included James and Dawes (both based in Tyseley) and New Hudson (Icknield Street).

One reason for Birmingham's dominance was its expertise in making steel tubing, the basis of bike frames. Another was the presence of so many companies able to supply precision made components. These included the Midland Wheel Co. of Aston; Joseph Lucas, who supplied lights

and batteries; Dunlop, makers of tyres (*see opposite*); JA Phillips of Smethwick, who manufactured frames, mudguards, pedals and handlebars; Perry & Co., the chain makers of Tyseley, and JB Brooks of Great Charles Street (*above*), who by the 1930s supplied 60 per cent of all saddles made in Britain.

Today the Brooks brand lives on in Smethwick, but under Italian ownership and with production overseas, while the city's last bike maker, Dawes, now based in Castle Bromwich, switched to design and distribution in 2002. As for Hercules, its name was bought up in 1960 by Raleigh, whose own Nottingham factory finally ceased producing bicycles in 1999.

An early 1930s worker reveals the contents of one of the millions of golf balls produced at Fort Dunlop – the rubber casing, composition filling, tapes for winding, rubber thread and a quantity of gutta percha. Golf ball production had begun at the company's Aston Cross works in 1908. Once at Fort Dunlop, tennis balls were also produced in vast quantities.

◀ It takes six people and four hours processing to make each **Acme Thunderer** whistle at the Barr Street factory of **Joseph Hudson & Co.** in Hockley. Nine styles are currently available. Around half are metal, the rest being polycarbonate. Most retail at between £3.50–4.50.

Precisely when a whistle was first used for football is not known – early referees had to officiate by waving a handkerchief or shouting – though research suggests that it may have been in Nottingham during the early 1870s (rather than, as is often stated, at a Forest v. Sheffield Norfolk game in 1878).

What is certain is that Joseph Hudson, a Derbyshire born tool maker of St Marks Street, Hockley, who had begun making whistles in 1870, was the first man to add the 'pea', or rather a cork ball, thereby increasing the whistle's power. He did this in response to a general plea from the Metropolitan Police in 1883, for alternatives to the wooden rattles traditionally used by bobbies on the beat.

Legend has it that Hudson hatched the idea after he dropped his much loved violin by accident. The jarring sound of the breaking strings set him thinking as to how such a discordant sound might be reproduced in a whistle.

The added pea, it transpired, was the answer.

The Metropolitan Police were delighted. Demonstrated on Clapham Common, Hudson's new 'cylindrical airfast whistle' could be heard over a mile away, and, just as importantly, could be blown hands-free whilst in full chase.

The police immediately ordered 21,000 whistles and have been customers of Hudson's ever since, as have police forces, navies and numerous other public services in 140 countries around the world.

Hudson was a hands-on boss, initially testing every whistle personally (a job now done by an air compressor). From 1888 his son Clifford, a keen ornithologist, also oversaw the introduction of various bird calls, a range still popular with hunters, dog trainers and musicians today.

Joseph Hudson himself died in 1930, but the Barr Street factory (*above*), built in 1910, remains a hive of hands-on craftsmanship in the best traditions of the Jewellery Quarter, with over 60 staff and sales of around four million whistles per annum.

Indeed, that a peep from any one of those whistles has the power to make or break the dreams of players, coaches and fans across the globe – from the humblest of pitches to the greatest of arenas – may well represent Birmingham's single most important contribution to the world of sport.

This brass Acme Thunderer, dating from between 1884–98, is one of many historic whistles in the Hudson's collection. A typical Thunderer produces a sound of 4,500Hz, while an average-sized sports crowd generates 3,800Hz. Not bad for a few ounces of metal and a cork 'pea'.

▲ One of several firms to capitalise on the popularity of billiards during the Victorian era was **Thomas Padmore & Sons**, whose staff are shown here in a 1930s brochure, fashioning pocket plates and rest heads at the company's Billiard Works on Edmund Street.

Originally from London, Thomas Padmore had set up as a wood and ivory turner and cabinet maker in Birmingham's Little Charles Street in 1830. By 1871 growing demand for the company's billiard tables persuaded his sons, John and Edwin, to move to Edmund Street, where, after an agreement on standards for billiard equipment in 1892, they expanded the range.

Using waste left over from the production of ivory billiard balls, Padmore's also produced car door fittings, bracelets, salt and pepper pots, and even truncheons.

When Birmingham staged the world's first snooker championships in 1927, in a billiard hall in John Bright Street, it is highly likely that a Padmore table was used. But snooker was then only in its infancy. The real prize was to be selected as a supplier for the World

Billiards Championships, which Padmore's finally achieved for the 1933 event, held at Dorland Hall, Lower Regent Street, when it beat off competition from its two London rivals, Thurston's and Burroughes & Watts. A further coup, and no doubt a costly one, was to gain an endorsement from Walter Lindrum, the Australian World Champion and Don Bradman of billiards (*below*).

Padmore tables were also supplied under government contract to outposts across the empire, until their Edmund Street works was

bombed during World War Two and manufacture was thereafter limited to accessories. Finally, in 1966 Padmore's was absorbed into the Liverpool-based Clare group, since when the company has acted as retailers only, on Lichfield Road, Aston (although it remains in the hands of the Padmore family).

This leaves one local company still making tables – Birmingham Billiards Ltd., originally set up in James Watt Street, Birmingham, in 1936, by WA Camkin (*see page 122*) and now based in Walsall.

Workers at Chad Valley prepare dartboards for sale in the late 1930s. Originally a stationery and printing firm called Johnson Brothers, the toys and games manufacturer adopted the Chad Valley name after moving to Harborne in 1897. (Chad Brook is a tributary of the River Rea.) At its peak in the 1950s over 1,000 people were employed, but production ceased in 1972 and the site is now Chad Valley Close. (Woolworth's subsequently bought the brand name.) The dartboards shown here are the familiar London Trebles boards, which won out over other regional designs when darts started to gain popularity during the 1920s.

As selected by Walter Lindrum for his Private Billiards Room.
Was also selected for the Championship of the World Match, 1933.

Chapter Twelve

Bowls

Ready for play at the Bournville Bowls Club, Mary Vale Road, formed in 1930 and one of 154 bowling clubs affiliated in the Birmingham area. It is estimated that there are some 6,000 active bowlers in the region, and although this number had dropped since the 1960s, there are signs of a recent revival.

Having focused on specific areas, and themes, we now turn to individual sports.

Long before the likes of cricket, football and lawn tennis caught on during the 19th century, bowls was in effect the national game. Southampton and Chesterfield claim to have greens established in the 1290s, while from the 16th century onwards – in addition to the story of Francis Drake playing on as the Armada approached in 1588 – come numerous references to bowls, including several in the works of Shakespeare.

Here was a game played in both towns and villages, by lords and labourers alike, by nuns and wives (Mrs Pepys included), and even on the occasional Sunday by John Knox and John Calvin.

But bowls was no genteel sport. To clamp down on the widespread betting and heavy drinking that accompanied games, and to ensure that men would not neglect their archery practice, Henry VIII prohibited the keeping of bowling greens for gain, allowing only those owning land worth £100 to maintain one for their own use.

Commoners were confined to playing at Christmas, and only then in their masters' grounds.

By the 17th century, however, the game was firmly back in fashion, for all social classes.

In the Birmingham area, at the top end of the scale, Aston Hall's green was laid out, probably around the same time as the building's completion in 1635, while for visitors to the weekly market in Solihull, the green at the George Hotel (then called The Bell) – which is still in use (*see page 110*) – may also date from the late 17th century, if not earlier.

In Birmingham itself the first greens appear on a map of 1731.

One, north of New Street, near to a cherry orchard, was owned by a Mr Corbet. By 1750 it had been taken over by Mr Packwood, and in 1792 is described as the green of the Union Tavern, Cherry Street. A second, unnamed green was situated at the junction of Summer Hill Terrace and Powell Street.

At least three further greens would open during the 18th century. Meredith's Bowling Green on Easy Hill (near where Baskerville House stands) is shown on a map of 1750, and

There are few more picturesque settings for bowls in Birmingham than the unusual L-shaped green at The Bell Inn, Old Church Lane, Harborne. Overlooked by the 17th century tower of St Peter's Church, the green dates back to at least the 19th century.

by 1778 was called Southall's. The Salutation Bowling Green occupied the corner of Summer Lane and Snow Hill (next to the General Hospital).

On New Street, the Hen and Chickens boasted a 'very good bowling green' in 1791.

By 1811, just outside the town, another green existed at the Vauxhall Gardens, Duddeston, where musical entertainments and a cockpit were also advertised.

The general tone of all these establishments, each licensed to sell ale, can easily be imagined. But in any case, the sites they occupied were worth far more to developers, and in their wake a new type of green emerged on the fringes of the town. An early example of this was the green and quoits ground laid out on the corner of Highfield Road and Harborne Road, Edgbaston, in 1825, for 'select members only'.

The advent of railways, and the drawing up of an agreed set of rules (by a Glasgow solicitor in 1849) also paved the way for clubs to form and to compete in organised tournaments.

In addition, as noted in Chapter Nine, bowling greens turned out to be just the right size to slot into the rapidly emerging pattern of suburban residential areas. Moreover, to play bowls one did need to be fit, or to invest in special equipment.

Recognising this, Birmingham breweries soon rediscovered bowling as a means of attracting business, a trend that continued until the 1930s, when a new breed of 'Reformed' pubs, many with greens at the back, opened up in Birmingham's suburbs.

At the same time Birmingham Corporation laid out greens in most of its public parks.

Companies did the same at their works grounds (*see Chapter Eight*).

But by the 1960s the boom was over. Dozens of pub greens, no longer able to pay their way, or with their clubs' membership in decline, were sold for development or converted into car parks. Companies decided that green maintenance, which requires specialist skills, was too costly, while a number of private clubs simply caved in when offers from developers proved too tempting for their members to resist.

A further indication of decline was that the number of municipal greens fell from over 30 in 1978 to fewer than ten in 2006.

That said, there are still more privately owned bowling greens in the Birmingham area than there are venues for any other sport. At a national level, moreover, bowls is currently Britain's fifth most popular participation sport, with some 600,000 registered players.

There are also signs of a revival. Modern forms of the game, such as indoor bowls played on artificial surfaces, plus the breaking down of gender barriers, have helped to attract younger players. Bowls is even encouraged at certain schools. Meanwhile, in the Birmingham area, new or restored greens have recently appeared at Marsh Lane, Solihull, the Tally Ho! Club, Edgbaston, Woodlands Park, Bournville and at The Maggies pub, Hall Green.

Bowls may no longer be the national game, therefore, but in the overall context of our sporting heritage, it forms a vital link with our past, as well as playing an important ongoing social role too.

After at least 700 years of bowls in Britain, and perhaps 400 years in the Birmingham area, the game is by no means up yet.

Abandoned during the 1930s, the bowling green at the now derelict Duke of York pub in Key Hill, Hockley, is the last surviving green in central Birmingham. The trees and high walls enclosing the green appear on a map of 1858, when the pub was known as the Old Tree Inn, but it is possible that the green may date back earlier, to the 1790s.

▲ Hidden from public view in Solihull town centre lies what is almost certainly the region's oldest functioning sportscape.

Although claims that the bowling green at **The George Hotel** is one of Britain's oldest are as yet unproven, we do know that the earliest, half-timbered elements of the building – now part of the Ramada Jarvis Hotel – date from the 16th century, and that the site of the green as we know it today became the inn's property in 1693. The only evidence that there may have been a green there at that time, or earlier, is that facing the green on the west side is a yew tree, trained into the shape of an arbour. According to a local history written in 1930, botanists were sure that this arbour (*seen above on the centre of the green's left side*) dated back to the 14th century.

But of course this offers no proof that the green is as old.

Instead, the first written evidence of its existence appears in August 1790, when the *Gentleman's Magazine* noted the death of Wm James, 'assistant to the Bowling Green at Solihull, Warwick'. It then added this curio: 'The bearers of his corpse by the last particular request of the deceased, played a game of bowls upon the green, on their return from the funeral.'

A year later came a newspaper report of a notorious public row that had broken out in 1783 at the 'Solihull Bowling Green' between Dr. Parr, Curate of Hatton in Warwickshire, and the Rev Charles Curtis, Rector of St Martin's in the Bull Ring.

In the 19th century the bowling green itself became something of a talking point when a topiarist trimmed the arbour into the shape of a peacock, the emblem of the Solihull Bowling Club, which had formed during the 1800s.

Today the club has over 100 members, but alas none appears to be handy with the shears and the peacock has lost its shape.

Another distinctive feature of the green remains unchanged however – the 15th century spire of St Alphege's, rising imperiously behind the hotel (*above*).

The church, it may be noted, is listed Grade I. The George Hotel is Grade II. But the green itself has no statutory protection other than the fact that it falls within a conservation area.

That it might ever be built upon is therefore unlikely. But how much better protected the green would be were it, and other greens of similar vintage, to be placed on English Heritage's Register of Historic Parks and Gardens.

▲ At first glance the scene at the **Tally Ho! Bowling Club** on Priory Road, Edgbaston, appears typical. But notice that the bowlers in the foreground are dressed casually, while those on the lower green are in whites. Also, play on the near green is taking place diagonally, while in the distance it is proceeding in a straight line.

The reason for these differences is that two different codes are being played; crown green in the foreground, flat (or level) green in the background.

The distinction between the two codes is both simple and complex.

Flat green bowlers play under the aegis of the English Bowls Association, formed in 1903 by cricketing legend WG Grace. Just as rugby split into Union and League in 1895, so too did the formation of the EBA cause a schism in bowls.

Flat green is concentrated in the south of England, the north east and Scotland. Crown green is largely confined to the Midlands, Lancashire and Yorkshire.

Crown green bowlers dress informally, behave informally, enjoy a bet, and play in any direction on greens, which typically rise in the centre between 9 and 15 inches. Flat green bowlers play in strictly divided sectors, called rinks.

The spiritual home of crown green bowling is Blackpool. For flat green it is Worthing.

For this reason, it is hardly surprising that the only clubs where the two codes are played on greens adjoining each other are both in BIrmingham, on the very border between the two territories.

The Tally Ho! Club is the first. The other, as it happens, lies just a few hundred yards away at the West Midlands Police Sports Ground on Pershore Road.

Despite the close proximity of both crown and flat green facilities, relatively few bowlers play both codes. But in Birmingham crown green predominates, with 141 clubs affiliated to the local counties bowling association, compared with just ten flat green clubs in the equivalent region of the EBA.

▲ In the heart of Longbridge territory – at least until the giant car plant closed in 2005 – **The Black Horse**, on Bristol Road South, Northfield, is a superb example of a 'Reformed' public house; that is, one designed to improve the image of the brewing industry by attracting a better class of drinkers and, just as importantly, their wives. In today's parlance we would call it a 'family pub'.

Opened in 1929 and designed in mock-Tudor style by Francis Goldsbrough (a specialist pub architect of the Arts and Crafts school), The Black Horse retains its original, wood panelled bars and lounges, with a positively baronial function hall at first floor level.

At the rear, overlooked by the hall's windows and its imposing pitched roof, is the crown green bowling green, spied here through a decorously overgrown gap in one of the rustic-style colonnades that flank two sides of the playing area.

Unusually, the bowls club pavilion includes a cellar, and also features wooden roof tiles, which, in common with the grounds and gardens in general, strongly merit sensitive restoration.

Other notable examples of inter-war Reformed pubs with bowling greens are to be found at the King George V, also in Northfield, on Bristol Road South (now a restaurant), and at the British Oak, Pershore Road, Stirchley.

◀ In 2005, the vandalised bowling green at **The Maggies Pub**, Shirley Road, Hall Green, was a sight all too familiar to Britain's bowling community. Here, surely, was yet another green destined to become a car park or block of flats.

Opened as The Three Magpies in 1935 and, along with The Baldwin on nearby Baldwin Lane, one of a pair of Moderne style brown brick pubs designed by the much respected EF Reynolds, The Maggies had itself closed in 1998, leaving the bowls club to struggle on alone until finally giving up the ghost two years later.

But all was not lost. Firstly, together with the pub, the bowls pavilion had, in 1997, been listed Grade II (making it the most modern of only five 20th century bowls-related structures to be listed). Also, it transpired that the green was protected from development by a covenant.

Then, in 2001, the pub was restored and reopened by its new owners, Greene King.

Still, the green's future looked bleak, until in 2005, a mile and a half northwards, another pub green, at The Greet Inn, Warwick Road, was sold for development.

For the dispossessed members of the Greet Inn Bowling Club, the forlorn green at The Maggies offered an ideal alternative.

Restoring the green and pavilion would cost the newly constituted Greet Maggies Bowling Club (*left*) over £4,000, and many hours of voluntary labour. But the result is much to their credit and, in April 2006 the club was able to enter seven teams into local leagues – yet one more example of how community sports clubs contribute not only to the nation's social fabric, but in many cases act as guardians of our built heritage too.

Chapter Thirteen

Lawn Tennis

Unveiled in 1982 by the Lawn Tennis Association and now a place of pilgrimage for tennis stars and aficionados from around the globe, the blue plaque at number 8 Ampton Road, Edgbaston, marks the site of what is generally agreed to be the birthplace of lawn tennis (although some evidence suggests that the first experimental games were played there in 1859 or 1860 rather than 1865, as stated on the plaque). The lawns from that period still exist to the rear of the house, which itself was built in 1855 by one of the players, Augurio Perera, a Spanish merchant who had moved to the city in 1839 at the age of 17.

Birmingham may justly claim to be the cradle of lawn tennis. But, as so often in sporting history, the story of how that came about is subject to varying interpretations.

By way of background, a diverse range of racquet sports are played around Europe, of which in Britain the longest established – nowadays called real, or royal tennis (to distinguish it from lawn tennis) – is played across a net in a high-walled court into which various voids and protusions have been added as extra challenges.

Britain's oldest surviving real tennis court, at Falkland Palace in Scotland, dates from 1539, followed by Hampton Court, built in 1625. Remarkably, both remain in use today.

No records exist of a real tennis court in Birmingham. Henry VII is known to have played at Kenilworth Castle in 1492. Other courts were built at Coombe Abbey, near Coventry, in 1820, and Hewell Grange, Redditch, in 1821. Even today Birmingham's nearest functioning courts are at Leamington Spa (b.1846) and Moreton Morell (1905).

One of the most important factors in determining how real tennis is played is the fabric of the ball. Since the game originated in medieval France the balls have always been handmade, using tightly wound cloth and various forms of stuffing. To achieve any bounce with such a ball required courts to have tiled floors and, ideally, roofs, to keep both balls and players dry. Inevitably, such courts were expensive to build, which is why real tennis has traditionally been an elite sport.

As for the lower orders, more impromptu forms of handball, played on the street or against church walls, were the nearest equivalents to real tennis, at least until the law intervened. In 1420, for example, handball was banned from the cloisters at Atherstone, while four years later players in Tamworth were threatened with imprisonment.

A number of innovations during the early Victorian period paved the way for lawn tennis to develop from these medieval games.

Affordable lawnmowers, first developed in the 1830s, made it possible for a much wider sector of society to maintain smooth swathes of turf within their own grounds or gardens.

This in turn created the conditions under which croquet, a game introduced from Ireland in the 1850s, could take root.

Edgbaston, with its detached villas set in spacious gardens, proved an ideal setting for the game to catch on amongst the district's socialites. Indeed croquet became, after archery, the first sport that respectable women were allowed to play in mixed company.

Another ball game to arrive in Birmingham was racquets (or rackets). Instead of players facing each other across a net, this was played against a wall (as in modern day squash). Unusually, rackets originated in two London prisons in the mid 18th century, where it was devised as a means of exercise.

The game reached Birmingham in the 1820s, when, according to tennis historian Lord Aberdare, a court was set up at the Islington, near Pie Bridge – a location not since identified – and in 1828 this hosted the first national rackets

A ladies tournament at the Edgbaston Archery and Lawn Tennis Society grounds in 1908. Alas, after fires in 1925 and 1964 there are no buildings of interest at the club. However the grass courts seen here are those that were first used in 1873, and indeed remain in use today. This almost certainly makes them the oldest lawn tennis courts in the world.

championships; the Londoner Thomas Pittman beating Thomas Butler from Birmingham.

A more formal Racket Court was then established c. 1849 on Bath Street, and it was here that the two men who would later claim to have invented lawn tennis would become friends.

TH 'Harry' Gem (1819-81), was a well known local solicitor and sportsman. JBA Perera, three years Gem's junior, was a Spanish merchant who had prospered sufficiently to construct a house, called 'Fairlight', on Ampton Road, Edgbaston, in 1855. Naturally, it had a croquet lawn.

What happened next was later retold by Gem in a letter to *The Field* magazine, in 1874. That year, a Major Walter Clopton Wingfield had patented a new game which he called *Sphairistike* (from the Greek for ball game), or Lawn Tennis. In its first year over one thousand boxed sets were sold, mostly to upper class families who were now bored with croquet and only too happy to find a new use for their lawns. (Wingfield himself was very much part of the country house set, being a close associate of the Prince of Wales.)

By his own account, Wingfield claimed to have started trials of his new game in early 1873.

To which Harry Gem, in his letter to *The Field*, riposted that he and Perera had been playing a very similar game for some fifteen years.

The pair, it emerged, had used standard rackets, but, rather than real tennis balls, they tried air-filled rubber balls instead.

Such balls, newly imported from Germany, were the direct result of another technological breakthrough: the vulcanisation of rubber, discovered by an American, Charles Goodyear, in 1839. Crucially, unlike real tennis balls, rubber balls bounced on turf.

In deference to Perera's Spanish roots, the two friends called their new game *pelota* (a Spanish ball game). But, it must be said, neither made any special effort to disseminate the game beyond their immediate circle, other than the fact that when both moved to Leamington in 1872 they soon recruited two doctors, members of the local real tennis club, to make up a foursome, and set up a court on the croquet lawn at the Manor House Hotel on Avenue Road.

It was there, in the summer of 1872, that the four men formed the world's first lawn tennis club.

Weeks later, in September 1872, a second club, the Solihull Tennis Society, established itself on Homer Road, Solihull.

Only in February 1874, nearly two years later, would Wingfield's tennis sets appear on the market.

Back in Edgbaston, meanwhile, tennis converts were keen to organise too, so that by 1875 – the year that lawn tennis was first played at the Marylebone Cricket Club and at the All England Croquet Club at Wimbledon – both the Priory Lawn Tennis Club (*see page 117*) and the Edgbaston Archery and Croquet Society, were up and running.

The latter club is of particular significance. Established purely for archery in March 1860, croquet was introduced in 1870. But once tennis arrived, in 1873, croquet's days were numbered, and in 1877 the club was restyled as the Edgbaston Archery and Lawn Tennis Society (EALTS). In fact archery ceased in 1925, but the name has been left unchanged.

Where exactly the society was first based is not known. But it is recorded that they moved to their present site – originally part of the Botanical Gardens – in 1867.

(Because both the Leamington and Solihull clubs have moved from their original homes, this makes EALTS the world's oldest surviving tennis club still playing on its original grounds.)

Within two decades lawn tennis had swept the nation. By 1890 it was said that no respectable house in Edgbaston was without a tennis lawn. By the 1920s, hardly a suburb in the city was without a club. Courts were also laid out at public parks, from 1883 onwards.

And to feed the demand, from 1918 until the 1950s, millions of balls were manufactured at Fort Dunlop in Erdington.

Tennis remains an important part of Birmingham's sporting culture. Over the years a number of international events have been staged. In the 1990s this included Davis Cup matches at the NIA (since lawns are now only one of several surfaces used in the sport).

At grassroots level too; in 2006, 46 indoor and outdoor clubs and centres were active in the region.

Gem and Perera's legacy, it would seem, lives on.

▲ Edge of the seat action during a Davis Cup match between Sune Malmstrøm and Henning Muller of Sweden, and Colin Gregory and Leslie Godfree of Great Britain, on a shale court at the **Tally Ho! Tennis Club**, Edgbaston, in May 1927.

In the background can be seen the roof of the stand and pavilion at the Edgbaston County Cricket Ground, across Edgbaston Road.

Laid out initially in 1907 by the Harborne Polo Club, the Tally Ho! was one of three local clubs able to host international tennis events.

The others were the Priory (*see opposite*), and the Edgbaston Lawn Tennis Club, on Edgbaston Park Road. The ELTC had formed in 1878, and in 1924 built a centre court with 3,000 seats. But in 1964, just as the club was

about to expand, its landlords, the Calthorpe Estate, decided to effect a merger between the ELTC and the Priory, but on the Priory site, with the Edgbaston Park Road site redeveloped as halls of residence.

For the Tally Ho! Club the axe fell in 1990 when its lease expired and members decamped, also to the Priory. The site was finally redeveloped in 2006.

With nearly 3,000 members, Birmingham's largest private sports club is the **Edgbaston Priory Club**, on Priory Road, a complex which, though discreetly hidden behind a belt of trees, features a total of 29 tennis courts (12 all-weather, 10 grass, four clay and three indoor); 10 squash courts (one of which is also used for racquetball), indoor and outdoor swimming pools, a gym, health spa, bars and lounges.

In the centre right of the aerial view can also be seen the neighbouring **Tally Ho! Bowls Club** (*see page 111*), which until 1990 shared facilities with the Tally Ho! Tennis Club on Edgbaston Road.

The bowls club's relocation was part of a series of moves that, as mentioned opposite, has also seen three tennis clubs amalgamating on the Priory Road site.

Sandwiched between the grass courts and all-weather courts at the Edgbaston Priory is a charming, half-timbered pavilion (*below left*), thought to date back to the early 1880s, when the Priory Lawn Tennis Club (founded in 1875), moved to the site from its original base on the corner of Pebble Mill Road and Pershore Road. If its vintage can be verified, it may well be the oldest operational sports building in Birmingham.

Otherwise the main clubhouse, which replaced a 1926 pavilion destroyed by fire, dates from 1967.

▲ Russian starlet Maria Sharapova holds up the **Maud Watson Trophy** after winning the 2004 DFS Classic – one of the leading grass court tournaments on the women's circuit – at the Edgbaston Priory Club. She also won it the following year, when a record 12,500 spectators attended the week long event.

Previous winners since 1982 include Billie Jean King, Martina Navratilova and Pam Shriver.

Maud Watson had herself been presented with the elegant trophy after winning the first two Ladies' Singles championships at Wimbledon in 1884 and 1885.

A vicar's daughter, Watson had caused quite a stir with her ankle length dress, rather a contrast with the relatively skimpy outfit (*below*) worn by Birmingham's only home-grown Wimbledon champion, Ann Jones, in 1969, and now on display in the Priory pavilion.

Chapter Fourteen

Horse Racing

For many years the winning post of Bromford Bridge racecourse – which saw its last race in June 1965 – was displayed near the shops on Bromford Drive, within yards of its original location (a house occupies the exact spot). The post now stands sentinel over a children's playground called The Starting Point, a hundred yards due west along Bromford Drive. In the distance can be seen an elevated section of the M6.

Few photos of Bromford Bridge survive. This rare view of the betting booths and grandstand was taken in September 1965 when virtually every fixture and fitting was sold at auction. Even the stand was sold, to Hednesford Raceway stock car circuit, near Cannock, where it stood until being torched by vandals in 1990.

There are 59 racecourses in Britain, but only a handful – including those at Newcastle, York, Nottingham, Leicester and Aintree – are located either in, or close to, our larger cities.

Since the legalisation of betting shops in 1961, a combination of declining revenues and rising land values has led to the closure of racecourses in Manchester (1963) and Lincoln (1964), together with London's last two suburban courses, Hurst Park (1962) and Alexandra Park (1970).

Joining that sombre list, in June 1965, was Birmingham's last racecourse, Bromford Bridge, thus bringing to an end 225 years of racing in Birmingham and leaving Warwick, Stratford and Wolverhampton as the closest courses still in business.

Birmingham racing historians Chris Pitt and Chas Hammond (see Links) have discovered that during those 225 years over 40 sites in the area have staged races at one time or another.

The first recorded meeting took place over three days in May 1740, and though the precise venue is unknown, entries were declared at The Swan Inn at Snow Hill. The same hostelry was used seven years later for a Whit Monday meeting advertised in *Aris's Birmingham Gazette*, offering a £50 purse. Between 1776 and about 1792, racing also took place at Bromsgrove, Lewd Heath (Solihull), and Wednesbury.

But the period when meetings were organised most frequently, in locations spread right across the region, was from 1835-95.

With only a few exceptions, the courses were marked out across fields or open ground rented especially for the meeting, with grandstands, beer tents, gambling booths and railings erected only on a temporary basis. And yet often these meetings drew considerable crowds, with estimates from 10,000 up to 30,000 being common. A race day could bring the whole town to a halt as the roads clogged with traffic and swarms of day trippers.

From 1835–40, for example, two-day meetings were staged on a mile long course near Olton Reservoir, with a grandstand directly opposite The Seven Stars pub. A crowd of 10,000 attended in 1836, but the stakes were too low, and the horses of insufficient quality to sustain interest – a complaint that would frequently be made at other meetings in the area over the following century.

Meanwhile, Birmingham's first steeplechase – that is, run across country with fences, ditches and water jumps – took place in March 1836 on a 3.5 mile course marked out by red and yellow flags on Barr Beacon, Great Barr. The *Sutton Coldfield Observer* reported, 'a most excellent day's sport to a very numerous assemblage.'

Other steeplechases, run at Urthwood Heath, Kings Norton, in April 1836, and Northfield, in 1849, turned out to be one-offs.

From 1850–72 the Birmingham Hunt also staged races at »

◄ The Packington Chase reaches a climax at **Bromford Bridge** in January 1956. Other races staged at the course in its 70 year history included the Bournville Handicap and the Elmdon Hurdle. (Indeed the fences were constructed from gorse collected in Elmdon).

Looking out from the grandstand towards Fort Dunlop (*right of the results board, in the distance*) and the Bromford Wire Mills, Bromford Bridge hardly appears scenic. Indeed the track ran within feet of the London Midland Railway line.

After the failure of Four Oaks Park in 1889 moreover, Bromford's creation in 1895 (by the Ford brothers, who had also developed Nottingham's Colwick Park), seemed an immense risk.

Yet Charles Richardson, writing in *The English Turf,* called Bromford 'the perfect model of what a course ought to be. The racing, and in particular the finishes, can be better seen at Birmingham than at many places.' It was also easy to reach, with its own railway halt and special buses laid on from town.

Ruff's *Guide to the Turf* noted that 'after Newmarket, it is undoubtedly the best straight course in the United Kingdom.'

In 1949 The Birmingham Racecourse Company purchased the 180 acre course for £81,855 and spent a further £35,000 on improvements in the late 1950s. These included building a bar which, at 334 feet, was apparently the longest in the world.

But after three years of repeated cancellations caused by poor weather, and with attendances down to around 5,000, in 1964 the board proved unable to resist an offer of £1.25 million from the City Council, who needed the land for housing as part of their post-war slum clearance programme.

Played in Birmingham **119**

▲ Compared with Bromford Bridge, **Shirley Park Racecourse**, on Monkspath Street (now the A34 Stratford Road), was a modest affair. Shown here is the paddock, in 1951, with the two wooden grandstands in the background illustrating how basic racecourse architecture could be at the lower end of the scale (at least before safety standards were introduced in the 1970s).

When it opened in 1899 Shirley became Birmingham's third course (along with Bromford and Hall Green, which was only three miles away). By the 1930s it was staging a full programme of National Hunt meetings, so popular that express trains would stop at Knowle and Dorridge to pick up racegoers returning to London.

But the war would end National Hunt racing at Shirley – and at a number of other smaller courses – and so in 1947 it became one of four courses in Britain to start staging races under the auspices of the Pony Turf Club rules (that is, with undersized horses). At a time when seemingly any sports event attracted a bumper crowd, Shirley managed to draw attendances of 15,000, with special buses laid on from the Bull Ring and outlying towns. Yet only seven years later the course was sold and redeveloped as the Shirley Golf Club, whose clubhouse (see page 90) now occupies the site of the old wooden grandstand (below).

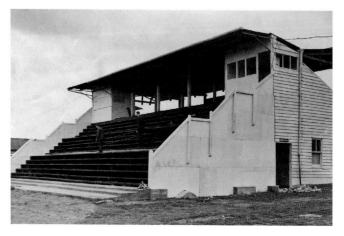

venues in Bickenhill, Knowle and Henley. None of these locations was easy to reach from Birmingham, however, and so in 1855 it was decided to hold the annual steeplechase closer to home, in Aston Park.

A circular course was laid out on the park's south side, alongside Victoria Road, with a grandstand bought from Coventry erected by the Great Pool (see page 45).

Racecourses had long been a magnet for nefarious characters. But at Aston Park on March 26 1855, the estimated 16,000 crowd would witness violence and intimidation of the sort associated with mods and rockers or football hooligans, a century or more later.

At one point in the fighting several jockeys refused to leave the weighing room. By the end of the meeting, reported the *Birmingham Mercury*, an estimated 11,000 riff-raff, some armed with ripped-up fence posts as bludgeons, had divided into gangs of 'British' and 'Russians', in a macabre re-enactment of the Battle of Alma, recently fought in the Crimea.

The violence then spread into the town centre, with mobs rioting in Dale End, Newtown Row and Summer Row. Sixteen people were hospitalised and three later sent to prison.

Unsurprisingly, the steeplechase returned to Knowle the year after.

But other races were staged in Birmingham over the next 40 years, including at Harborne, Handsworth (where Handsworth Park would later be laid out), Sparkbrook (where punters could also enjoy an 'exhibition of educated monkeys'), Smethwick and at Small Heath, where, in 1880 there took place possibly Britain's first ever ladies only race, albeit with just two entries.

But it was to the north of the town that the first semi permanent courses appeared.

Moor Hall racecourse, by Moor Hall Park, was home to the Birmingham Steeplechase from 1857–73, during which time the opening of the Birmingham to Sutton railway in 1862 helped boost attendances to between 25-30,000. The highlight of these meetings was the Birmingham Grand Annual, an event deemed second only in importance to the Grand National.

Despite this, the Moor Hall course fell victim to urban encroachment by the mid 1870s.

As noted in Chapter Five, Sutton Park was another focal point for racing between 1830 and 1879, most notably at Holly Knoll (which had a permanent grandstand), and at Longmoor Valley.

Only with the demise of this last venue would the Birmingham area gain its first permanent racecourse.

Situated just beyond the park's boundary in the grounds of Four Oaks Hall, Four Oaks Park opened in 1881 and featured paddocks, stables, offices and five stands (*shown on page 56*), the largest of which held 3,000 spectators.

Designed along similar lines to Kempton Park and the fashionable Parisian track of Auteuil, it was built by Surman & Sons of Great Colmore Street and was the first local course to cater for both Flat racing and National Hunt.

But for all its finesse, and despite the opening, in 1884, of Four Oaks railway station, crowds and purses quickly dwindled, and by the time the course closed in 1889, even the Birmingham Grand Annual, which Four Oaks Park had taken over, had been reduced to a two-horse race worth a mere £80.

Rather more enduring was the May meeting held in Hall Green, from 1871–1910, and once more in 1918, on land bordered by Shirley Road and Lakey Lane, and shared with Robin Hood Golf Club.

At its peak, crowds of up to 30,000 would flock to Hall Green for 'Nailcasters Derby Day' (nail making being a popular local cottage industry).

But, ultimately, only two courses would survive beyond 1918: Bromford Bridge, opened in 1895, and Shirley Park, which lasted from 1899–1954.

It is now over 40 years since Bromford staged its last race, the longest unbroken hiatus since racing began in 1740. But it is one that, given the economic realities of modern racing, seems certain to continue indefinitely.

Instead, local racegoers must take themselves to Warwick, Stratford or Wolverhampton.

▲ The most vivid reminder that the Bromford Estate was built on the site of Birmingham's best loved and most enduring racecourse, is this open space at **Stratford Walk**, which retains the exact oval shape of the former paddock, and even its steel boundary posts, thought to date back to the course's refit in the late 1950s.

Otherwise, various estate roads are named after racecourses (such as Newmarket Way, Haydock Close and Cheltenham Drive) or after race horses (Reynoldstown Road, Tulyar Close and Arkle Croft). At the eastern end of Bromford Drive there is also The Racecourse pub.

Regrettably, the colours and saddle of Bromford's last ever winner (on 21 June 1965), formerly displayed at The Saddle and Boot pub (now the Bromford Bridge Members Social Club), disappeared in the 1990s, and so, apart from the winning post (*see page 118*), precious few artefacts from Bromford Bridge survive.

Chapter Fifteen

Billiards

As if to warn all those who fail to notice the signs saying 'Strictly Members Only', a pair of crossed cues marks the entrance of the Frames 6 Snooker Hall on Soho Road, Handsworth, one of several opened in the Birmingham area during the Edwardian period by the Willie Holt chain of billiard halls, based in Burnley.

In common with most British towns and cities, Birmingham possesses a number of interesting billiard halls. But almost the last thing one would expect to see in one of them is someone actually playing billiards.

Rather, the majority will be playing snooker – an offshoot of billiards, invented by British Army officers in India in 1875 – or pool, a more recent introduction from America, played on smaller tables.

Billiards, which is thought to have originated in medieval France as a game played on the ground – *billart* means a mace, or cue, in Norman French – first achieved popularity in aristocratic circles after it had been converted into an indoor, table-based activity.

Britain's first billiard hall opened in London in the 1790s, and by 1801 Joseph Strutt, in his epic tome on British games and pursuits (*see Links*), saw fit to describe billiards as 'so generally known' that further elucidation was deemed unnecessary.

As the 19th century wore on, a series of innovations, such as the introduction of slate beds in 1826, and vulcanised rubber cushions in 1849, led to the standard form of table used today. By 1914 halls existed in every town and city. But more than that, in country houses, Edgbaston villas, smart hotels, Reformed pubs, sports clubs, even in prisons and sanatoriums, the provision of a billiard room had become practically *de rigueur*.

Rival manufacturers sent out legions of salesmen to spread the gospel, selling not only tables and equipment but also the lifestyle. For the average man, billiard halls offered a seductively lit refuge from the outside world. For hustlers and loafers, the smoke-filled den became a second home.

Two Birmingham companies capitalised on this appeal; Thomas Padmore & Sons of Edmund Street (*see page 107*), and Birmingham Billiards Ltd, on James Watt Street. The latter was owned by a leading figure in Birmingham sporting circles, Bill Camkin.

In the 1920s Camkin befriended a young billiards professional called Joe Davis, from Derbyshire. Billiards, sensed Davis, was losing its popularity. Leading players such as the Australian Walter Lindrum (sponsored by Padmore), were clocking up huge scores. For most spectators the rules had become too complex.

Instead, Davis noticed, people grew far more animated when professionals finished off their evening at the billiard table with a quick display of snooker, regarded by the purists as little more than a frivolous game for amateurs.

So it was, at Bill Camkin's behest, that the world's first snooker championships were staged in Birmingham, at his company's flagship outlet, the Camkin Rooms, on John Bright Street, from May 9–12 1927.

Joe Davis was the winner (as he would be every year until 1946), and by the end of the decade, billiards had been all but eclipsed. (Bill Camkin meanwhile went on to be Birmingham City honorary manager during World War Two.)

Since then snooker has gone global, thanks to colour television, but in pubs and halls has come under threat from pool, which is quicker and easier to play, using tables half the size.

▲ No less than their counterparts in the cinema industry, British billiard companies vied with each other to construct palatial exteriors for their flagship halls.

This fine brick and terracotta example, on **St Michael Street, West Bromwich**, was designed by local architect Albert Bye for the Willie Holt billiard company (owners of the Handsworth hall seen opposite). Opened in August 1913, beyond its narrow lobby area lay a clear spanned hall measuring 160 x 42 feet, sufficient for 20 full size tables and three smaller ones for beginners.

As was the norm, the side and back walls – tiled to a height of nine feet – were windowless, with glazed panels in the roof providing the only natural lighting.

Entrance was free, and only non-intoxicating drinks and tobacco were served. Around the walls were 150 raised seats for onlookers.

Alas, none of the original interior fittings survive, following the hall's conversion into a JD Wetherspoon pub in 1998. But of four former Willie Holt saloons surviving in the Birmingham area, the quality of its exterior is quite unmatched.

▶ Another hall built for the Willie Holt billiard company during the Edwardian period was this two storey example on **Walford Road, Sparkbrook**, still in use today, although with its original interiors either removed or concealed behind modern panelling.

Unlike snooker, which is played with a total of 22 balls, billiards requires only three, hence the three ball motif above the door (*repeated also on the examples shown on both previous pages*).

And now the hall is the sole survivor of a triumvirate of early 20th century leisure buildings which once occupied this end of Walford Road, handily placed for Stratford Road and the Number 8 Inner Circle bus route.

The other two, both operated for a period by the great showman and entrepreneur Pat Collins, were the Waldorf Cinema (appropriately, if anagramatically, named, given its address) – outside which the comedian Sid Field learnt his trade as a busker – and the Empire Roller Skating Rink, of which more in the next chapter.

▶ Not all side doors at branches of **Montague Burton** – the self-styled 'Tailor of Taste' – were as grand as this one on the corner of Bristol Road and North Road, Selly Oak. But their very existence signified only one thing – the presence of a billiard room on the first floor.

Burton, a Jewish refugee who started out as a pedlar in Chesterfield in 1900, ended up owning a chain of some 600 stores. Many were designed by the company architect from 1928–38, N Martin and, wherever possible, incorporated billiard rooms in order to attract working class men who, in the 1920s at least, were not used to shopping for clothes.

Burton was undoubtedly in tune with popular culture. Press coverage of the exploits of Joe Davis and his brother Fred turned snooker into a national craze in the late 1920s and early 1930s.

Thus customers would be fitted for their suit, and then directed to the tables upstairs whilst the necessary adjustments were made.

Former Burton stores are easy to spot, especially in places like Selly Oak, where the 1937 foundation stone survives. But only two Burton's billiard rooms still operate locally: on the corner of Stratford Road and St John's Road, Sparkhill, and above the Sutton Coldfield branch on Lower Parade.

◀ Readers familiar with cinema architecture might immediately spot a resemblance between this 1930s billiard hall and the iconic Odeon Cinema on King's Road, Kingstanding, designed by Birmingham architect Harry W Weedon in 1935.

In fact the billiard hall is located only a stone's throw away, on **Kingstanding Road**, and with its white, curved front bay contrasting sharply with the brick screen wall behind, it is patently a miniaturised version of the cinema. Even the stepped up central brick pillars echo the rather grander three fins of the Odeon's tower.

Once inside the billiard hall, now called Maximum's, all comparisons with the cinema must end. Façade apart, this is a functional building of no great merit. But at least it is still in use for snooker, whereas the cinema is now a bingo hall.

At the time of the billiard hall's opening, there were 46 similar establishments listed in the city. In 2006 there were 35, with a total membership of around 20,000 enthusiasts.

This 1930s mahogany and brass scoreboard – made by Thomas Padmore & Sons of Edmund Street – is still in use at Billesley Community Fire Station on Brook Lane, Moseley. Note that the upper and lower rollers were designed to mark up scores for both billiards and snooker, with sliding panels in between for scoring 'life pool' (a game unrelated to modern day American pool). This board allows for up to eight life pool players; that is, four on either side of the central slate, each being allocated a colour and three lives. The board originally cost ten guineas, plus four guineas for the open fronted ball box below.

Chapter Sixteen

Skating

Changes in the ice hockey world happen almost as rapidly as they occur on the ice. Based at the Solihull Ice Rink, which opened in 1965, the Solihull Barons are the latest of several clubs to represent the area. Others have included the Birmingham Maple Leafs, in the mid 1930s, and more recently the Eagles and Rockets. The Barons themselves were once known as the Solihull Blaze. Apart from the Barons, four amateur ice hockey clubs are based at Solihull (the Vikings, Vipers, Wolves and Vixens), plus a speed skating team (the Mohawks) and two figure skating and ice dancing clubs. In a busy week over 10,000 people use the rink, the only one now operating in the Birmingham area.

In the days before both climate change and concerns for health and safety conspired to make natural ice a rare and dangerous commodity, Birmingham's wealth of pools, ponds, lakes and canals ensured that Brummies were never short of places to skate when winter set in.

George and Richard Cadbury would often skate for an hour or two on St Martin's Pool at Bournville before heading to the factory, while Sutton Park's pools and Edgbaston Reservoir were also popular gathering points.

In this chapter however, we focus on purpose-built facilities for skating, both on ice and on roller skates.

Since the 18th century there had been various attempts around Europe to design a practical roller skate so that enthusiasts might skate all year round. But, as with lawn tennis and billiards, the breakthrough only came once improvements had been made both to the equipment and to the quality of available surfaces.

The first occurred in 1863, when an American, James Plimpton,

invented the first four wheeled roller skate that enabled users to change direction. This was followed by the development of modern asphalt, which allowed for the provision of smooth, hard wearing surfaces.

'Rincomania' – as the resultant roller skating craze was dubbed – arrived in Birmingham in the mid 1870s, some nine years after the world's first rink opened in Rhode Island.

One of the first rinks was next to Edgbaston Reservoir. Described as a 'very fine skating rink and entertainment hall', the Edgbaston Roller Rink featured daily musical accompaniment from the band of the Royal Staffordshire Blues.

Between 1875–78 eight other rinks opened around the city: at the newly expanded Aston Lower Grounds (*below*), Bingley Hall, Curzon Hall, Handsworth, Rotten Park, St James' Hall (on Snow Street), and on Navigation Street, where the City Rink was linked to

a Winter Garden. In Moseley a Mr W Dyke Wilkinson opened a rink behind the Trafalgar pub (where numbers 124–140 Woodbridge Road now stand).

Despite efforts to maintain interest by staging novelty races and roller football, few of these rinks would survive, and only one more opened before the end of the century, at the Sherbourne Hotel, Balsall Heath, in 1887. Rinking was expensive. Entry cost 6d, plus another 6d for skate hire.

On the other hand, roller skates were now being mass produced in an improved and lighter form, partly thanks to the incorporation of a new type of wheel axle, with ball, or roller bearings, that had been patented in Birmingham by William Bown of Summer Lane and a gifted 27 year old tool maker, Joseph Henry Hughes. Indeed it might even be said that not only roller skating but modern day skateboarding owes a great deal to this pair's ingenuity. »

The first roller rinks, such as this one at the Aston Lower Grounds, opened in 1878, were little more than gas-lit sheds. Strict rules required everyone to skate in the same direction and not to stop, 'except to assist a lady'. As this promotional sketch from the Lower Grounds guidebook was keen to show, rinks were ideal for ladies and children, and for courting.

◄ The story of the **Erdington Roller Skating Rink**, on the corner of Orphanage Road and Edwards Road – where there is now a fire station – is no doubt typical of many roller rinks built during Britain's second bout of 'Rincomania' between 1900–14.

Costing £5,000 and barely more than a corrugated shed – largely because its initial licence was only for seven years – the rink was designed by Charles Bosworth and was described as identical to another one on Monument Road.

Inside, the walls were lined with matchboarding, with a café by the entrance and accommodation for 350–400 spectators on five rows of seating around three sides of the rink. The rink itself, made from maple, measured 169 x 75 feet.

Like most of its counterparts, Erdington's rink soon struggled, and in 1911 part of the building was converted into a cinema. Only a curtain divided audiences from the skaters (and this was in the era of silent films).

The business ceased in 1918 and in 1929 the unwanted hulk was conveniently destroyed by fire.

A different fate awaited the **Edgbaston Roller Skating Rink** (*left*). When it closed in the 1920s the rink was converted into the Tower Ballroom, a building which, much altered, would survive until 2006.

▲ Wembley may have had its twin towers, but from 1910 until the early 1980s, Sparkbrook was noted for the twin turrets of the **Empire Roller Rink**, **Walford Road**.

Standing adjacent to the Willie Holt Billiard Hall (*see page 124*) and the Waldorf Cinema, for a period the rink formed part of the entertainments empire of the noted fairground operator, Pat Collins.

Opened as the Empire Skating Palace, the building was claimed to be the largest covered roller rink in Europe, with a maple floor measuring just under 200 x 100 feet (large enough to fit in seven tennis courts). Equally impressive was its clear spanning, timber barrel roof – of the type known as a Belfast roof – which again may have been one of the largest of its type ever built.

While the majority of roller rinks did not last beyond the 1920s,

the Empire, which in 1929 was grandly renamed the **Embassy Sportsdrome and Exhibition Hall**, enjoyed a revival in the 1960s.

On Saturday nights, crowds of up to 3,000 revellers would attend rollerskate discos, during which the music would periodically stop to enable the staging of speed skating races by the debonair **Birmingham Eagles**, whose members included world speed record holder Leon Goodchild, and world champion Leo Eason.

But by far the biggest draw was boxing, with crowds as large as 9,000 cheering on such British fighters as Randolph Turpin (the first black world champion, from Leamington, in the 1950s) and, in the 1960s, Birmingham's own heavyweight hero, Johnny Prescott.

Also appearing at the Embassy in concert were Louis Armstrong, the Kaye Sisters and Screaming

Lord Sutch (who apparently was booked in preference to another up and coming act called The Beatles).

But it was not boxing, music or even rising juvenile delinquency that put paid to roller skating at the Embassy. Instead, the opening of the Silver Blades Ice Rink in town persuaded the leisure operators Mecca Ltd to convert the now redundant ice rink on Summer Hill Road (*see opposite*) into a modern roller rink.

This in turn led to the Embassy being leased out for the much less troublesome, and more profitable, business of bingo.

This phase lasted until the 1970s, and although there were plans to develop the structure into a sports centre, the Embassy spent its final days as a warehouse, until a fire razed it to the ground in the early 1980s.

Housing now occupies the site.

» Once again, however, it took further improvements to the floor surface before roller skating could undergo its next popular phase. A new generation of roller rinks started appearing in the early 20th century using maple floors instead of asphalt. These were more durable, springier and warmer underfoot, and could also double up as dance floors.

Between 1900 and 1914, at least 450 of these improved roller rinks opened up around Britain, of which ten have been noted in the Birmingham area; including Aston, Northfield, Erdington, Smethwick and two in West Bromwich. One, on Monument Road, was part of the American Roller Rink chain, while Sparkbrook could boast what was considered to be the largest roller rink in Europe (*see left*).

Few of Birmingham's rinks survived beyond the 1920s, but Sparkbrook outlived the Second World War, and only in the late 1990s did the city's last survivor – Ronnies Roller Rink, housed in the former Empress Cinema on Witton Lane, Aston – finally close.

But that is not the end of the story. During the 1960s and 1970s there existed an informal asphalt circuit, snaking around a factory complex in Melchett Road, Kings Norton, where the National Skating Federation's British team trials were staged. Roller skating sessions are also held at certain local authority leisure centres in the region, such as Fox Hollies.

In addition, Birmingham can lay claim to having the nation's only purpose-built, outdoor speed skating track, at the Wheels Adventure Park in Saltley, where race meetings and training sessions take place for Britain's latest generation of roller skaters.

In 1967 Birmingham's 'Olympic Rolarena' (the former Birmingham Ice Rink) became the first British venue to stage the World Roller Skating Championships. In the lobby was a barber's shop, handily placed to trim the hair of any youth whose appearance was not to the management's approval.

▲ Although experimental indoor ice rinks had appeared in Britain as early as the 1870s – a story detailed in *Played in Manchester* (see Links) – it was not until some years later that refrigeration techniques had been sufficiently honed for investors to try again.

A freezing winter in 1929 also helped to remind the public 'what good fun skating is' (as the directors of Birmingham's proposed rink were careful to emphasise).

Designed by Sydney Clough and opened in September 1931 at a cost of £100,000, the **Birmingham Ice Rink**, on the corner of Summer Hill Road and Goodman Street, Ladywood, was one of 19 built in Britain between 1929–35.

Alas, few images of it survive, and those that do, such as this view from the 1930s, rather fail to back up the rink's billing as 'the St Moritz of the Midlands'.

Externally, it was a building of no merit (in contrast to several of its contemporaries elsewhere in Britain). Internally, it had an ice pad measuring 200 x 85 feet, sufficient for 1,000 skaters.

Two of its best known users were Olympic Gold medallist John Curry, who trained there as a teenager, and Olympic speed skater Wilf O'Reilly, a member of the Mohawks team, then based at the rink.

By the 1960s, Mecca Ltd, the rink's operators, decided that Ladywood no longer provided a welcoming environment, and so in 1964 a replacement, the **Silver Blades** (*right*), designed by the noted architect John Madin, was built on Pershore Street.

Meanwhile, the old ice rink was converted into a plush roller rink, a venture which lasted only seven years. A car showroom now occupies the site.

As to the Silver Blades, after being revamped as Planet Ice in 1997, the rink closed after a fire in 2004. Solihull, one of 60 rinks still open in Britain, is therefore the only rink currently operating in the Birmingham area.

Chapter Seventeen

Swimming

Over a century after its completion in 1902, the glowing red brick and terracotta entrance to the Men's Second Class Baths at Green Lane, Small Heath – a building now used as a Muslim community centre – exemplifies the use of diverse materials and styles, and the attention to detail that characterises Birmingham's exceptional stock of historic swimming baths from the first half of the 20th century.

Birmingham's affinity with water, detailed in Chapter Ten, extends also to its provision of public bathing, washing and swimming facilities. Indeed the city can lay claim to a range of historic swimming pools that is arguably unsurpassed in Britain.

Firstly, of some 80 public indoor baths in Britain that are listed, six are in the Birmingham area, including Moseley Road Baths, which is one of only four given the higher ranking of Grade II*.

Secondly, of the 20 public baths still operating within the city's boundaries, seven were built before 1939, of which three date from before 1914. These are Woodcock Street Baths (1902), now owned by Aston University, Tiverton Road (1906), and the aforementioned Moseley Road (1907). No other city has three Edwardian pools still in use.

Thirdly, and no less importantly, for any student of 20th century architecture, Birmingham's surviving pool buildings span an unusually broad range of building styles, typical of the Edwardian era, the 1930s and the 1960s.

After encouraging reports from other municipalities, Birmingham's Baths Committee opened its first Turkish Baths – or 'Hot Air Lavatories' as they were originally titled – at the city's flagship Kent Street Baths in 1879. Others followed at Grove Lane (1907) and Erdington (1925). These steam rooms date from Kent Street's reconstruction in 1933.

Also to be found are interesting examples of how historic baths have been converted to other uses; for example, as flats, as a museum gallery and as a training centre.

Not that there is any room for complacency. In common with almost every other major urban authority, Birmingham faces a number of challenges in its stewardship of older baths. Vital, but significant expenditure needed for the conservation of Moseley Road, for example, has inevitably to be balanced against public demand for modern pools, not least a much needed 50 metre pool for both training and competition. (As of 2006, the nearest 50m pool to Birmingham is in Coventry.)

To complicate matters further, swimming is no minority interest. Instead, it is Britain's most popular physical recreation after walking. A public pool is therefore

considered a necessity rather than a luxury. Regular swimmers also feel strong loyalty towards their historic baths.

Such are the inherent tensions that it is rare for any closure to be accepted without protest, or for a new pool to open without implications for older facilities.

Birmingham's first recorded baths were, as in other parts of Britain, privately owned. The first, referred to on a 1731 map as the Cold Bath, and subsequently as the Ladywell Baths, was located in the vicinity of modern day Ladywell Walk, off Hurst Street.

Under the ownership of a Mr Munro, Ladywell Baths offered ten baths for men and women, two with hot water, and, set in a walled garden, a pool measuring 100' x 50'. As described in William West's *Topography of Warwickshire* (1830) patrons were waited on by 'respectable and obliging attendants'. There were also facilities for invalids, together with a separate bath for members of the Jewish synagogue that had opened in nearby Hurst Street in 1791.

In 1846 a second private bath opened in Balsall Heath, with a similarly sized open air pool, costing 10s 6d for a season or 6d per entry, and with private baths each costing 1s for admission.

The public funding of baths as we know it today also began in 1846, with the passing of the Baths and Wash-houses Act.

A response to growing concerns for the health and hygiene of Britain's rapidly expanding urban population, the Act gave local authorities the power to borrow public money to erect public washing and laundry facilities. Given the risks entailed, only eight authorities took immediate advantage, of which Birmingham was among the first.

In fact concerned Birmingham citizens had already formed a Public Baths Association in 1844 and, having raised over £6,000 for the cause, had purchased land close to the Ladywell Baths, on Kent Street, knowing that local underground springs would offer a plentiful water supply.

After the passing of the 1846 Act, this site was transferred to the ownership of the Town Council, who waited a further two years before sanctioning the start of building work.

Opened on May 12 1851, Kent Street Baths (see right), proved to be an expensive prototype, reaching £23,000 in costs after the foundations were repeatedly flooded by the underground springs. On the other hand, those springs, and many other aquifers around the region, were to provide

the Birmingham Baths Committee with a cheap and fresh source of water that was the envy of other cities, who mostly had to rely on supplies from the mains.

Kent Street's facilities were typical of their time. There were First and Second Class swimming pools, both reserved almost exclusively for men; a suite of 69 private 'slipper' baths (or individual baths for washing), three plunge baths, and a laundry, fitted with 25 basins and two sets of drying horses (or racks).

Within a year of Kent Street's opening the Baths Committee started planning a second set of baths, for the densely populated district of Duddeston. This led to the opening of the Woodock Street Baths on August 27 1860.

Baths on Northwood Street followed in 1862, serving the northern part of the town, and Monument Road, in 1883, on the west side. Over the next decade, further baths were built in the neighbouring boroughs of Smethwick (at Rolfe Street) and Aston (on Victoria Road).

Finding available sites with an accessible water supply was seldom straightforward, and it was only after years of debate and trial drillings that Birmingham's next phase of development began with two schemes, at Green Lane, Small Heath (1902) and Moseley Road, Balsall Heath (1907), in which the Baths Committee and the Free Libraries Committee combined facilities on the same site.

During this period further baths were built by Birmingham Corporation at Nechells (1910), by Handsworth Local Board at Grove Lane (1907), and by King's Norton and Northfield District Council at Tiverton Road (1906) and Bournville Lane (1911). »

▲ Few architects had any experience of designing indoor pools before the 1846 Baths and Wash-houses Act, which might explain why Birmingham's first public pool – opened at **Kent Street** in 1851 (top) – was a curious mixture of Queen Anne and Italianate styles, with red brick facings, bath stone dressings and decidely domestic proportions.

The building was replaced by the new Kent Street Baths in 1933.

Woodock Street Baths (above), opened in 1860, appeared more purely Italianate, with red brick facings on a blue brick plinth.

Both Woodcock Street and Kent Street contained residential accommodation for the baths superintendent and his family.

Although part of Woodcock Street – a pool added in 1902 – is still in use for swimming today, the building shown here was replaced in 1926.

These last three baths all came within Birmingham's jurisdiction after their respective councils were absorbed into greater Birmingham in June 1911.

Bournville Lane was also the first in the city to be fed from the mains and fitted with a modern water circulation and filtration system. (This ended the unseemly but commonplace practice by which pools were filled at the start of the week and emptied only several days later, with admission prices falling each day as the water grew murkier.)

Including the returns from various cottage baths built in the city's poorer districts – that is, smaller units housing only slipper baths and laundries, with no pools for swimming – attendances at Birmingham's baths exceeded one million for the first time in 1913, a figure that would continue to grow after the First World War.

To cater for demand, in 1923 almost identical structures were opened on Institute Road, King's Heath and Lordswood Road, Harborne, both built using labour provided by the Unemployment Relief Scheme. Baths on George Arthur Road, Saltley, followed in 1924, and on Mason Road, Erdington, the year after.

By this time, the city's Victorian baths were becoming increasingly outdated and unable to meet higher standards for water quality. Both Woodock Street (in the mid 1920s) and Kent Street (in the early 1930s) were therefore rebuilt, as was Monument Road, in 1940.

These redevelopments, together with baths opened at Sparkhill (1931), Northfield (1937) and Kingstanding (1938), featured varying degrees of Art Deco detailing and colour schemes, and layouts clearly influenced by the health spa movement emanating from Germany. Just across the city boundaries the Moderne style Smethwick Baths (1933) also represented a break from more traditional forms.

Swimming was by now hugely popular. By the late 1930s annual attendances regularly exceeded two million. Competitions, diving displays and water polo matches were attracting thousands of spectators to the city's main gala pools, at Kent Street, Moseley Road and to Saltley (which had the city's first 100 foot long pool). In 1933 alone, it was reported, approximately 100 galas took place in Birmingham, organised by dozens of local clubs. (The oldest of these, and indeed one of the oldest in Britain, was the Birmingham Amateur Swimming Club, founded at Kent Street in 1862, and later merged with the Leander Club, which had met at Northwood Street since 1877.)

Growth continued after the Second World War. Although two of the Corporation's open air pools, at Cannon Hill Park (*see page 29*) and Small Heath closed in early 1939 owing to new regulations regarding water quality, and Northwood Street closed in 1947, annual attendances peaked at three million in 1950.

But although the numbers stayed high, post war shifts in population, combined with slum clearances, required a further phase of construction in the 1960s.

Birmingham's first City Architect, AG Sheppard Fidler, oversaw the design of the first large scale suburban pool at Stechford, opened in 1962, followed by Newtown in 1969 and Beeches Road, Great Barr, in 1972.

Tudor Grange pool in Solihull dates from the same period.

Although these post war pools, designed as they were in the stripped, Modern style of the day, with box-like steel framed structures and plentiful glazing, appear not to have worn as well as their pre-war predecessors, those that would follow from the mid 1970s onwards are widely held to possess even less aesthetic value.

But this new generation of facilities no longer offered just swimming pools. Instead, they combined wet and dry sports within one site.

Thus, in 1975, the distinctive 1902 baths at Green Lane gave way to the anonymous Small Heath Leisure Centre on Muntz Street. The 1938 Kingstanding Baths was replaced by the metal-clad, warehouse-style Kingstanding Leisure Centre in 1988. King's Heath Baths (1923) was similarly superceded by the Cocks Moors Woods Leisure Centre.

This period also saw the introduction of irregularly shaped leisure or 'splash' pools, replacing the traditional rectangular tank with flumes, wave effects and beach-style fittings to attract family groups.

Another 1980s change in strategy saw the city's leisure department combine with the education committee to provide facilities shared by schools and the public. The first of these hybrids – an echo of the Edwardian link-up between baths and libraries – was the Fox Hollies Leisure Centre, opened in 1986 in Acocks Green.

And so the provision of public swimming facilities has moved through several distinct phases since the 1846 Act, each phase bequeathing buildings that encapsulate the concerns and fashions of the day.

In this context, Birmingham's historic pools add greatly to the depth and diversity of the city's historic environment.

Moreover, this is a tale that continues to evolve, so that while current concerns rightly focus on the fate of Woodcock Street and Moseley Road, questions have started to arise as to the future of the city's inter-war pools, notably Harborne. Indeed it may not be long before even those seemingly unloved examples from the 1960s and later will need to be re-evaluated in conservation terms.

Civic pride at Harborne Baths, Lordswood Road, one of two baths built by the Corporation during the 1920s that is still in use. Erdington is the other.

▲ Birmingham's oldest operating pool – and indeed one of the oldest in Britain – is the intimate and much treasured former First Class pool at **Woodcock Street Baths**, Gosta Green, opened in 1902. In common with other Birmingham baths of this period, it features studded terracotta ornamentation above each cubicle arch (*shown also on page 152*), and roof girders pierced with quatrefoil decoration.

Woodcock Street has been redeveloped twice since baths first opened on the site in 1860.

In 1902 the pool above was built on the same site as the slightly smaller original. Also added were First Class private baths and a steam laundry.

However, the bulk of the building as seen today, accessed via the Woodock Street entrance (*above right*), dates from a second major redevelopment, designed in the mid 1920s by Arthur McKewan. This saw the addition of a Gala Pool, measuring 100 x 35 feet, with seats for up to 1,100 spectators, extra private baths and a laundry.

When the baths were taken over by Aston University in the 1980s, ironically it was the older but smaller 1902 pool that was preserved, while the Gala Pool was converted into a sports hall.

Its pitched and top-lit roof can be seen in the centre of the complex (*left*), with the narrower 1902 pool immediately to its right. In the lower left hand corner, the former laundry is now a fitness centre.

Despite being listed Grade II, Woodcock Street's future now appears to depend on plans by Aston University to construct a larger multi-purpose sports complex elsewhere on the campus.

▶ Dominated by its intricately detailed, if now weed-infested clocktower, the **Small Heath Public Library and Baths**, Green Lane, is one of dozens of characteristic red brick and terracotta civic buildings – schools, libraries, offices and police stations – designed for the city by the firm of Martin & Chamberlain in the 19th century.

Small Heath was the first site on which both the Free Libraries and the Baths Committees agreed to combine, if only because it had taken 35 years to find a suitable site in the rapidly growing district. Even then Henry Martin's plans had to be pared down by omitting electric lighting and a spectators' gallery in the First Class Baths.

Opened finally in 1902, the apex of the site, defined by the clocktower, housed the library, with the First and Second Class Baths and wash-house filling the larger rear part of the triangular site.

War damage closed part of the baths from 1940 until the early 1950s. But the building would close altogether c.1977 when a desperately uninspiring modern library and pool complex opened in nearby Muntz Street.

Since then parts of the Grade II listed Green Street building have been successfully used as a Muslim community centre, although the condition of its fabric continues to cause concern.

▲ Only seven indoor swimming pools have been granted Grade II* status, of which three are still in use: the RAC Club, Pall Mall; the National Sports Centre, Crystal Palace; and, in Birmingham, the **Balsall Heath Public Baths**, on Moseley Road. This, therefore, is a building of national significance.

As at Small Heath, the baths were a joint venture with the city's Free Libraries Committee, although here, the library (*the section with the clocktower, to the right*), designed by Jethro A Cossins & Peacock, opened first in 1896, whereas the baths (*to the left*) followed in 1907 and were the work of architect William Hale & Son, and engineer Job Cox.

There are three entrances: for the Men's First and Second Class Baths, with a central doorway leading to the Women's Baths, above which is an heroic City Coat of Arms by Benjamin Cresswell. The two octagonal turrets act as ventilators to the male and female private slipper baths sections.

The Baths and Library form part of an intriguing cluster. Opposite is the Grade II* Moseley School of Art, and within walking distance may be found the Imperial Picture Palace, the Moseley & Balsall Heath Institute, the Moseley Tram Depot (now a skatepark) and the Society of Friends Hall & Institute.

Population trends and road changes may have forever altered the character of Moseley Road, but these precious buildings surely offer the best possible foundations for any potential renewal of civic pride.

▲ After the closure of the **Moseley Road Baths** for almost a year, the re-opening of the Second Class swimming pool, in October 2005, was greeted with great relief.

The smaller of two pools on the site – the First Class pool remains closed (*see opposite*) – the Second Class pool measures 71 x 33 feet and retains many original features, including its elliptical cast-iron roof supports, lantern roof, and white and blue glazed bricks. Modern cubicles have replaced the originals (which consisted of oak benches divided by hanging ceramic slabs and curtain fronts). Gone too are the leaded lights in the far windows and the diving stage at that end (removed for safety in the 1980s).

Delightful though the pool is, however, the £1 million worth of emergency repairs that were necessary to allow it to re-open – for example to the 110 foot chimney stack, the water filtration system, and to various structural elements – only scratched the surface of what needs to be done to restore the bulk of the baths and library fabric. In 2006 the likely cost of this programme was estimated at over £10 million.

▲ **Moseley Road Baths** is not only a place to swim, it is also the living repository of a lifestyle that was common to millions of Britons in the 20th century. Alas now closed, but still largely intact, are the men's private slipper baths, each in their own tiled cubicle (*top right*) with bell-pushes to summon extra hot water. Also rarely found in surviving Edwardian baths are the steam-heated drying racks in the former public laundry (*above right*).

But in truth, from the main entrance hall (*top left*) to the bath's furthest, dingiest corners, every detail of this building appears to have been thoughtfully engineered or crafted, using the finest materials of the day – glazed bricks, terrazzo flooring, ornate ironwork, leaded glass, oak doors and fittings.

All this splendour comes together most dramatically in the First Class, or Gala Pool (*above left*).

Regrettably now mothballed and awaiting vital repairs, the pool measures 81 x 32 feet, is bordered by 63 cubicles and overlooked by a three-sided spectator gallery and balconettes on the far wall.

Here is aqua-theatre at its very best. Here is a national treasure.

▶ Few Brummies have cause to pass along Kent Street nowadays, just a short distance from the bright lights of Hurst Street. And yet behind an unmarked, 170 feet long Portland stone Art Deco frontage between Wrentham Street and Gooch Street lies one of the forgotten treasures of Birmingham.

Kent Street Baths was the first, and for many years, the largest and most prestigious public baths in the city.

Setting a trend for all baths built in Birmingham before 1911, the original Kent Street baths, opened in 1851, were fed by underground springs (a mixed blessing as the builders struggled to keep water from the foundations). By 1897 the facilities included First and Second Class pools, First and Second Class private baths for men and women, a laundry and the city's first Turkish Baths. A separate Women's pool and extra private baths were then added in 1914, on the Gooch Street corner (where a redbrick building, *seen right*, now stands).

This last addition would be the only part of the baths left standing when construction of the baths as we see them today began in 1930.

Designed by Archibald Hurley Robinson, architect also of Sparkhill Baths (*see page 140*) and re-opened in May 1933, the new Kent Street Baths was a starkly modern, reinforced concrete water palace, very much of its time. At its heart was the 100 x 34½ feet Gala Pool (*above right*), with an Art Deco diving stage centred under a back-lit proscenium arch, and ventilation ducts operated by electric motors.

As at Sparkhill, Hurley Robinson lined all interior walls with glazed bricks in primrose, set off by black banding, except in the Russian Baths and Turkish Baths (*see page 130*), where green predominated.

The new baths' heyday proved to be shortlived. Bomb damage to the Gala Pool closed the building from 1940–46, and although its facilities were still advanced, as the immediate area became depopulated after the war demand fell and the baths closed in 1977.

Since re-titled Kent House and listed Grade B by the City Council, subsequent uses have included a workshop and showroom. But as of 2006 the building stood empty and seemingly beleaguered as all around it redevelopment beckons.

Externally Kent Street Baths have worn well. Internally the state of its former facilities is unknown.

A Saturday night dance in 1933 at **Saltley Baths**, George Arthur Road (opened 1924, demolished 1995). Until the 1950s it was common for pools to be boarded over during the winter to save water heating costs.

In Birmingham this trend started at Northwood Street Baths in 1905 at the behest of the newly formed Social Institutes Committee, whose aim was to offer 'recreation of the broadest and most comprehensive character, on neutral ground, for both sexes, unassociated with any sect or political party'.

Billiards, bagatelle, cards, chess, draughts and rifle ranges were offered at seven public baths initially. But from the 1920s onwards, cheaply priced weekend dances and whist drives proved by far the most popular. In 1948, it was reported, the Corporation's Baths Department (the Social Institutes Committee having disbanded in 1945) catered for over 5,000 dancers per week at Kingstanding, Harborne, Saltley and Moseley Road, with badminton also on offer at King's Heath and indoor bowls at Grove Lane.

Opened in 1933, the Grade II listed Smethwick Baths, Thimblemill Road, were designed by Chester Button and Smethwick Borough Engineer, Roland Fletcher. With its concrete arched Gala Pool and spectator galleries, Art Deco mosaic detailing, original brass fittings, doors, signage and steel casement windows, this is a rare example of a still functioning 1930s Moderne pool (albeit one facing substantial remedial work by its operators, the Sandwell Leisure Trust). From 1956–59 the baths staged international swimming matches v France, Sweden and East Germany.

▲ Opened in 1931 and still in use today, **Sparkhill Baths**, Stratford Road, was the work of Archibald Hurley Robinson, who also designed Kent Street Baths and several local cinemas (such as the ABC Bristol Road, in 1937). After touring various modern baths around Europe, Hurley Robinson opted at Sparkhill for a spa-like, top-lit interior (*right*), sub-divided by a colonnade and with no pool-side cubicles. Noticeably sparcer than earlier designs, the use of oak, pine and walnut, combined with soft colours, notably primrose, helped create a calmer ambience.

The baths at Monument Road (*above right*), opened 1940 and demolished 1994, and Northfield (*right*), opened 1937 and still extant, echoed Sparkhill's Art Deco interior but with more traditional exteriors. Reflecting changing social provision, Northfield (by architect HW Simister) offered mixed bathing, a café, car park, but no private washing facilities.

▲ Birmingham's first pool of the post war era was also the first to have been designed by the newly established City Architect's department, set up in 1953 by the Modernist, AG Sheppard Fidler.

Set in landscaped grounds, **Stechford Baths**, Station Road (*above left*) opened in 1962 and, in contrast to its more introspective predecessors, used extensive glazing to create a light and airy interior, seen here in its original state, devoid of the clutter which has accrued since the entrance was extended in 1991. Stechford's outdoor pool (*top left*), the last built by the city, was also redeveloped in 1991, with the Cascades leisure pool now occupying the site.

Other examples of the Modern style are **Newtown Pool**, designed in 1969 by R Seifert and Partners (*above right*), and **Beeches Road Pool**, Great Barr (*top right*) by City Architect Alan Maudsley, dating from 1972.

Both pools remain in use, and despite garnering little affection, each nevertheless exudes a purity that appears to be lacking in the 'crinkly tin' leisure centres that followed in the 1980s.

There are dozens of boarded up and decaying historic swimming baths across Britain, their loss keenly felt, their fate uncertain. One such example in Birmingham is the Grade II listed Bournville Lane Baths, Stirchley, by John P Osborne. Built in 1910–11 on land gifted by the Cadbury family, and closed in 1988, it stands only a few hundred yards away from the Cadbury factory's Girls' Baths (*see page 36*), which is itself also decommissioned. In 2006 hopes were raised that, even if the Bournville Lane Baths are not to be restored to use, the building may be converted into some form of community centre, along the lines of Nechells (*see opposite*).

▲ The vexed issue of how historic baths might be adapted to other uses has been answered in various ways within the Birmingham area.

Grove Lane Baths, Handsworth (b.1907) has been converted into flats. Green Lane Baths, Small Heath (*see page 134*) is now a Muslim community centre.

Rolfe Street Baths, Smethwick, has been preserved in a quite different manner, however. Built in 1888 and closed in 1989, the baths were dismantled, brick by brick, and re-erected at the Black Country Living Museum, Dudley, where the roof structures now span exhibition halls. Note how the iron girders echo those still in use at Woodcock Street (see *page 133*).

Of equal interest is the recent refurbishment of the Grade II listed

Nechells Baths, on the corner of Nechells Park Road and Aston Church Road (*see opposite*).

Opened in 1910 and designed by Arthur Harrison, the baths closed in 1995 and gathered dust until, in 2003, the Birmingham Foundation (a charity formed by local businesses) purchased the building from the Council for £5.

Since then, the Foundation, in conjunction with the Nechells Regeneration Project, has overseen a £4 million building programme, jointly funded by the City Council, the Heritage Lottery Fund, the European Development Fund, the employment agency Pertemps and Advantage West Midlands.

Reopened to the public in early 2006, the baths now house an Enterprise and Community Centre.

In addition to retaining the Edwardian façade, the interior layout and fabric has been carefully retained, albeit with subtly harmonious additions. The former slipper baths now act as meeting rooms. The pool area contains the offices of the Pertemps agency, with the dressing cubicles converted into storerooms. Other facilities include a crèche, internet-café, training rooms and workshop studios.

Arguably, the baths might have offered greater benefits to the community had its swimming facilities been restored. But as has been found so often elsewhere, such was the level of corrosion to structural elements and services that the costs would have been considerably greater than the £4 million eventually expended.

The transformation of Nechells Baths was carried out by TPS Consult in conjunction with Christopher Thomas Architects and Linford Bridgeman Construction. The addition of a mezzanine floor over the main pool (*left*) has increased available floorspace by 45 per cent, leaving the roof structure intact, while tiled walls and cubicles have been preserved at ground floor level. New entrances and extensions have been sited at the rear of the baths, leaving the original Nechells Park Road twin-turreted entrance (*above left*) intact. The building is one of several Birmingham baths that will feature in *Great Lengths*, a study of historic indoor pools to be published as part of the *Played in Britain* series (*see Links*).

Chapter Eighteen

Conclusions

In 1913 a young author was at Cheltenham to see Gloucestershire play Warwickshire, one of whose bowlers had a distinctive action. Three years later, pondering a name for one of his characters, he recalled the bowler, and the name stuck. The bowler's identity? Percy Jeeves. The author? PG Wodehouse. This is the county cap worn by Jeeves in 1914, his last season before being killed at the Somme in 1916. It is now on display at the Edgbaston museum, the only sports museum in the Birmingham area. The bear and ragged staff on the cap derive from the Warwickshire coat of arms.

It was the snobbish Mrs Elton – a character in *Emma*, Jane Austen's novel of 1814 – who famously said of Birmingham, '... not a place to promise much, you know... One has not great hopes from Birmingham.'

In common with so many casual critics of the city, we can be sure that the woman had never visited. Indeed Birmingham has always confounded expectations, and never more so than in the field of sporting heritage.

As the 2002 *Played in Britain* study of Manchester also found, even local experts have expressed surprise at the depth and diversity of what has been discovered in Birmingham and its surrounds.

Here, clearly, is a city which has much to celebrate from its sporting past.

But while we hope that *Played in Birmingham* will be informative, the book should not be regarded as an end in itself. Rather, our study has raised a number of issues that relate not only to Birmingham's sporting heritage, but which are of relevance to the nation's sporting past as a whole.

Many of these issues are too complex to be summed up in a few sentences. Nevertheless, it is hoped that the brief points which follow will draw attention to those that raise most concern.

Historic sports buildings

In common with all buildings and structures of historic or architectural significance, buildings for sport are already eligible for protection under the current system of listing.

Indeed several listed buildings are featured within this book.

There are, however, a number of unlisted buildings which, as a result of this study, may merit consideration. Candidates include the Rowheath Pavilion, Bournville (*see page 39*), The Barn, Manor Farm Park (*page 41*), the Magnet Centre (*page 77*), the clubhouse of Shirley Golf Club and pavilion of King Edwards's School (*both page 90*), the pavilion and colonnade at The Black Horse bowling green (*page 112*), the tennis pavilion at the Edgbaston Priory Club (*page 117*), the Billiard Hall, West Bromwich (*page 123*), Maximum's Snooker Club, Kingstanding (*page 125*) and Beeches Road Swimming Pool (*page 141*).

It will be interesting to see if readers feel strongly about other featured buildings.

Sports clubs and leisure providers have ever changing needs and listing is perceived by some as hampering both day-to-day management and long-term planning, whilst adding to overall costs. Any further listing of sports buildings therefore needs to be pursued in collaboration with those managing and using sports facilities, and be accompanied by suitable guidance and support.

Historic sports grounds

Sports grounds and open spaces enjoy a measure of protection under the government's Planning Policy Guidance Note 17 and, at a local level, under Unitary Development Plans. Some grounds also fall within conservation areas.

However, there are no specific mechanisms in place to provide added protection to sports grounds of historic significance.

One solution would be for these grounds to be included on the Register of Historic Parks and Gardens, which is maintained by English Heritage, and which in Birmingham has 17 sites, including the grounds of Aston Hall and Edgbaston Hall, both significant in sporting terms.

Candidates for inclusion on the Register are the gardens of 'Fairlight', 8 Ampton Road, Edgbaston (*see page 114*), where the first games of lawn tennis took place, the grounds of the Edgbaston Archery and Lawn Tennis Society (*page 115*), the bowling green of The George Hotel, Solihull (*page 110*) and the former paddock of Bromford Bridge racecourse (*page 121*).

Buildings at Risk
No-one associated with the management or use of Balsall Heath Baths on Moseley Road (*see page 135*) will need reminding of the building's worrying state of repair, its recent partial re-opening notwithstanding.

However, the importance of conserving this building cannot be over-emphasised. The baths are of considerable national importance, on a par, at the very least, with the Victoria Baths in Manchester, whose plight has received far greater media attention.

It is therefore recommended that some form of trust, or Friends group, be established to focus attention on the baths' current state and their future, not least so that those areas currently barred from the public may be made accessible on a controlled basis.

Maintaining historic buildings
Sports clubs in possession of historic properties currently gain no support on conservation issues from sporting bodies. We found many voluntary workers struggling to maintain buildings and grounds which form an integral part of the local scene, and often provide social outreach for elderly and disadvantaged members of the community.

Sporting bodies must share with organisations such as English Heritage, the Heritage Lottery Fund and local authorities, some of the responsibility for providing guidance and incentives for those clubs that act as unpaid guardians of our sporting heritage.

Museums and collections
At present only one museum in Birmingham specifically relates to sport – the museum of Warwickshire CCC at Edgbaston (*see opposite*). It is our view that there exists considerable scope for creating a publicly accessible collection of the city's sporting treasures, not least bringing together items, trophies and memorabilia relating to the Birmingham & District Works Amateur Football Association (*see Chapter Eight*), currently held in private storage.

It is also strongly urged that the necessary funding be secured to purchase the Albert Wilkes collection of photographs, currently in private ownership in London, for storage and conservation by the City of Birmingham Archive.

A further aspect of the city's heritage that merits consideration for a museum or visitor centre concerns the contribution of the Aston area to the development of sport in Birmingham, and in particular the heritage of Aston Villa and the role played by William McGregor in the foundation of the Football League.

Individual commemorations
There are current plans for the creation of a long overdue statue of William McGregor outside Villa Park. To this the Civic Society might consider a blue plaque marking the site of McGregor's shop in Summer Lane, where the first discussions took place for the formation of the Football League.

Other candidates for plaques include the site of the Birmingham Athletic Institute in John Bright Street (*see page 10*), The Reddings rugby football ground (*page 72*), the former headquarters of the Birmingham & District Works AFA, Stratford Road (*page 85*) and Kent Street Baths (*page 138*).

Of even higher priority should be the creation of a high profile memorial to honour George Cadbury, probably the single most important benefactor in the history of Birmingham sport and recreation. (A road named after Cadbury in Balsall Heath was retitled Mary Street following Cadbury's pacifist stance during the Boer War).

The lack of such a memorial constitutes a serious omission.

Birmingham schoolboys display their gymnastic talents for the camera in 1929 – one of thousands of images of local sporting activity recorded by the prolific photographer and former Aston Villa footballer, Albert Wilkes. The Wilkes collection, which spans the years c.1907–70. is currently held by a commercial agency in London. But its home should surely be in Birmingham, within the public realm.

Links

Where no publisher listed assume self-published by organisation or author

Where no publication date listed assume published on final date within title, ie. 1860–1960 means published 1960

Birmingham General

Birmingham City Council *Developing Birmingham: 100 Years of City Planning 1889–1989* Development Department
Chinn C *Brum and Brummies 2/3* Brewin Books (2001/02)
Dent RK *Old and New Birmingham, Vol 2, from 1760 to 1832* Houghton & Hammond (1880)
Foster A *Pevsner Architectural Guides: Birmingham* Yale University Press (2005)
Gil C *History of Birmingham Vol 1* Oxford University Press (1952)
Hopkins E *Birmingham, The First Manufacturing Town in the World* Weidenfeld & Nicholson (1989)
Hopkins E *Birmingham: The Making of the Second City 1850–1939* Tempus (2001)
Hutton W *An History of Birmingham* Pearson & Rollason (1783)
Langford JA *A Century of Birmingham Life, Vol 1* WG Moore & Co (1870)
Moseley Local History Society *The Listed Buildings of Moseley* (1989)
Noszlopy GT, ed Beach J *Public Sculpture of Birmingham including Sutton Coldfield* (1998)
Pugh RB (ed) *A History of the County of Warwickshire, Vol 17* University of London Institute of Historical Research (1964)
Skipp V *Victorian Birmingham* (1983)
Sutcliffe A & Smith R *Birmingham 1939–70, Vol III* Oxford University Press (1974)

Chapter 1. Played In Birmingham

Birmingham City Council *The National Stadium in Birmingham: A Unique Opportunity* (1994)
Jenkins C, Shoebridge M & Van Zyl P *The Birmingham Athletic Institute Remembered* Brewin Books (1992)
Galligan F *Gymnastic Activity in the West Midlands 1865–1918* University of Coventry D Phil Thesis (1999)
Langley T *Big Brum, The Gentle Giant* (1965)
Molyneux DD *The Development of Physical Recreation in the Birmingham District 1871–1892* University of Birmingham MA Thesis (1957)
Strutt J *The Sports and Pastimes of the People of England* Methuen (1801)
www.kabaddi.org
www.necgroup.co.uk/visitor/nia
www.birminghamwheelspark.org

Chapter 2. Edgbaston

Bannister J *The History of Warwickshire CCC* Christopher Helm (1990)
Brooke R *Cricket Grounds of Warwickshire* Association of Cricket Statisticians (1989)
Carr S *The History of The Birmingham Senior Cup Part One 1876-1905* Grorty Dick (1999)
Duckworth L *The Story of Warwickshire Cricket 1882-1972* Stanley Paul (1974)
Santall S *History of Warwickshire Cricket* Cricket & Sports (1911)
Plumptre G *Homes of Cricket: The First Class Grounds of England and Wales* MacDonald Queen Anne Press (1988)
Slater T *Edgbaston, A Brief History* Phillimore & Co (2002)
Trott T (ed) *King Edwards School, Birmingham* Tempus (2001)
www.calthorpe.co.uk
www.edgbastoncroquetclub.org.uk
www.edgbastongc.co.uk
www.thebears.co.uk
www.sport.bham.ac.uk

Chapter 3. Bournville

Brannan J & F *A Postcard from Bournville* Brewin Books (1992)
Bromhead J *George Cadbury's Contribution to Sport* The Sports Historian, Vol 20, No 1 (2000)
Broomfield M *A Bournville Assortment* W Sessions (1995)
Broomfield M & Denley J *Bournville, The Early Years* (2002)
Crosfield J *The Cadbury Family, Vol. 2*
Gardiner AG *The Life of George Cadbury* Cassell & Co. (1923)
Goodyear DW *Bournville Cricket Club: 1882-1982*
Gumbley E *Bournville: A Portrait of Cadbury's Garden Village in Old Picture Postcards* SB Publications (1991)
Hampson M (ed) *Bournville and Weoley Castle* Tempus (2001)
Harrison M *Bournville: Model Village to Garden Suburb* Phillimore (1999)
Chinn C *The Cadbury Story* Brewin Books (1998)
Rogers TB *A Century of Progress 1831-1931: A History of Cadbury Brothers* Cadbury (1931)
Wagner G *The Chocolate Conscience* Chatto & Windus (1987)
Williams I *The Firm of Cadbury 1831–1931* Constable
www.cadbury.co.uk
www.cadbury-club.co.uk
www.bvt.org.uk
www.rowheathpavilion.co.uk

Chapter 4. Tame Valley
Alexander Prof WO & Morgan W (eds) *The History of Birchfield Harriers 1877-1988*
Fairclough O *The Grand Old Mansion, the Holtes and their Successors at Aston Hall 1618–1864* Birmingham Museum and Art Gallery (1984)
Hodder M *Birmingham, The Hidden History* Tempus (2004)
Inglis S *Villa Park 100 Years* Sports Projects (1997)
Price VJ *Aston Remembered* Brewin Books (1989)
Twist M (ed) *Images of England: Aston and Perry Barr* Tempus (1999)
www.avfc.co.uk
www.perrybarrstadium.co.uk
www.birmingham.gov.uk/alexander.bcc
www.birchfieldharriers.net

Chapter 5. Sutton Coldfield
Bates S *Sutton Coldfield: A Pictorial History* Phillimore (1997)
Baxter M (ed) *Sutton Coldfield: The Archive Photographs Series:* Alan Sutton (1994)
Baxter M (ed) *Sutton Coldfield: The Archive Photographs Series: The Second Selection* Chalford (1997)
Baxter M & Field J *Sutton Coldfield, Then & Now* Tempus (2002)
Davies R & Gifford RC *Sutton Coldfield Golf Club 75th Anniversary 1889–1965*
Fletcher RF *Sutton Coldfield Golf Club 1889–1989*
Jones DV *The Royal Town of Sutton Coldfield, A Commemorative History* Westwood (1973)
Jones DV *Sutton Park: Its History and Wildlife* Westwood (1982)
Jones DV *Sutton Coldfield 1974–84* Westwood
Lea R (ed) *Scenes From Sutton's Past* Westwood (1989)
Lea R *The Story of Sutton Coldfield* Sutton (2003)
www.fospa.org Friends of Sutton Park
www.spmac.info Sutton Park Model Aero Club

Chapter 6. Moor Pool Estate
Chinn C *Brum and Brummies* Brewin Books (2000)
Hampson M *Images of England: Harborne – The Second Selection* Tempus (2002)
Harborne Tenants *Into the 1980s at Moor Pool* (1980)
McKenna J *Birmingham, The Building of a City* Tempus (2005)
www.moorpool.com
www.circletennis.net

Chapter 7. Stadiums and Grounds
Bamford R & Jarvis J *Homes of British Speedway* Tempus (2001)
Byrne M (ed) *Archive Photos Series: Hall Green* Chalford (1996)

Green MD *Images of England: Small Heath and Sparkbrook* Tempus (2002)
Inglis S *The Football Grounds of Britain* Collins Willow (1996)
Peel C *The Non-League Football Grounds of the West Midlands Past and Present* Newlands Printing Services (1996)
Fairn A *A History of Moseley* St Mary's, Moseley PCC (2003)
Reyburn R *Life at the Graveyard: Moseley Ashfield Cricket Club 1900–2000* Jones & Palmer
Woodrooffe P *The Reddings 1880–2000* Moseley (RU)FC
Moseley Football Club Centenary 1873–1973
www.bcfc.com
www.hallgreenstadium.co.uk
www.moorgreenfc.co.uk
www.moseleyrugby.co.uk
www.wychallwanderersjuniorfc.co.uk
www.sandwell.gov.uk/sports/sportsfacilities/hadley-stadium
www.wba.co.uk

Chapter 8. Works Grounds
Birmingham & District Works Amateur Football Association Golden Jubilee Souvenir 1905–55
Birmingham County FA Millennium Book 1976–2000
Chinn C *Birmingham, The Great Working City* Birmingham City Council Libraries (1994)
Davis AE *First in the Field: A History of the Birmingham & District Cricket League* Brewin Books (1988)
www.the-stadiumclub.com Transport Stadium
www.westmidlandspoliceclub.com

Chapter 9. Clubs and Pavilions
The Crowning Glory, Harborne CC 1868–1996 (1999)
Hiscox WC (ed) *Shirley Golf Club 1955–95* Regency Press
The Re-location of The Stone Moseley Ashfield Cricket Club, Moseley Football Club (Rugby Union) (2000)
www.kes.bham.sch.uk King Edward's School
www.moseleyashfieldcc.co.uk
www.moseleygolfclub.co.uk
www.moseleytennis.org
www.solsch.org.uk Solihull School

Chapter 10. Parks and Pools
Bartlam N *Britain in Old Photographs: Ladywood* Sutton (1999)
Birmingham Rowing Club *The Forward Oar Centenary Supplement* (1973)
Conway H *Public Parks* Shire Garden History (1996)
Foster WR *Factors in the Development of the Public Park in the West Midlands* Centre for Urban & Regional Studies (1974)
Hampson M (ed) *Images of England: Edgbaston* Tempus (1999)
Kilby T (ed) *The Centenary of Olton Mere Club: A History 1899–1999* Brewin Books (2000)

www.birmingham.gov.uk/parks
www.hags.co.uk/planet Kings Norton Wheeled Sports Park
www.leisure.birmingham.gov.uk
www.birmingham.gov.uk/leisurepoint
www.fer.org.uk Friends of Edgbaston Reservoir
www.midlandsailingclub.org.uk
www.baa.co.uk Birmingham Anglers Association
www.ghof.org.uk Get Hooked on Fishing

Chapter 11. Made In Birmingham
Bartleet HW *Bartleet's Bicycle Book* J Burrow & Co (1933)
Allen GC *The Industrial Development of Birmingham and the Black Country 1860–1927* Frank Cass (1966)
Cattell J, Ely S & Jones B *The Birmingham Jewellery Quarter: An Architectural Survey of the Manufactories* English Heritage (2002)
Cattell J & Hawkins B *The Birmingham Jewellery Quarter: An Introduction and Guide* English Heritage (2000)
Drake P & Baxter M *Images of England: Erdington Volume II* Tempus (2003)
Foster TJ *Whistle Wizards: Trusty Tales of Toil and Triumph* Acme Whistles (2002)
Mitchell JR (ed) *Billiards and Snooker: A Trade History* British Sports and Allied Industries Federation (1981)
Ryerson B *The Giants of Small Heath: The History of BSA* Haynes (1980)
Turner K *Images of England: Made In Birmingham* Tempus (2001)
www.acmewhistles.co.uk
www.brookssaddles.com
www.fattorini.co.uk
www.dunlopsports.com
www.thurston-games.co.uk
www.vmcc.net Vintage Motor Cycle Club

Chapter 12. Bowls
Bowls Club Directory 2001 PW Publishing (2001)
Cadbury Brothers Ltd *Our Birmingham: The Birmingham of our Forefathers and the Birmingham of our Grandsons* ULP (1943)
Castleton SH & D'Alton E *The Solihull Bowling Club* (1991)
Crawford A & Thorne R *Birmingham Pubs 1890–1939* The Centre for Urban and Regional Studies, University of Birmingham/Victorian Society Birmingham Group (1975)
Warwickshire & Worcestershire Counties Amateur Bowling Association *Official Manual 1968*
Warwickshire and Worcestershire Counties Amateur Bowling Association *Official Yearbook 2004*
www.bowls.org
www.bowlsengland.com
www.wwcba.com

Chapter 13. Lawn Tennis
Aberdare Lord *The JT Faber Book of Tennis and Rackets* Quiller Press (2001)
Elks SJ *From Whalebone to Lycra* (2005)
Gillmeister H *Tennis: A Cultural History* Leicester University Press (1997)
The Priory Lawn Tennis Club 1875–1964; The Edgbaston Priory Club 1964-1975 (2000)
www.edgbastonpriory.com
www.ealts.net
www.solihullarden.co.uk

Chapter 14. Horse Racing
Bates S *Shirley, A Pictorial History* Phillimore (1993)
Dixon C *Robin Hood Golf Club 1893-1993*
Pitt C *A Long Time Gone* Portway Press (1996)
Pitt C & Hammond C *When Birmingham Went Racing* CC Publishing (2005)
Woodall J *The Book of Greater Solihull* Barracuda (1990)
www.bromford-bridge.pwp.blueyonder.co.uk

Chapter 15. Billiards
Padmore *Billiard Tables by Padmore* brochure c. 1939
Sigsworth Eric M *Montague Burton, The Tailor of Taste* Manchester University Press (1990)
www.eaba.co.uk English Amateur Billiards Association
www.tradgames.org.uk

Chapter 16. Skating
Portrait of Birmingham City of Birmingham Information Department (1969)
Douglas A *Birmingham at Play* Brewin Books (1994)
Mayell L *The Birmingham I Remember* Lodenek Press (1980)
Clegg C & R *Picture Palaces of Birmingham & Solihull* (1984)
Pout R *The Early Years of English Roller Hockey 1885–1914* (1993)
Price VJ *Birmingham Cinema: Their Films and Stars 1900–60* Brewin Books (1986)
www.iceskating.org.uk
www.brsf.co.uk British Roller Sports Federation

Chapter 17. Swimming
Baxter M & Drake P *Images of England: Moseley, Balsall Heath and Highgate* Tempus (1996)
Green MD (ed) *Images of England: Kings Heath* Tempus (1998)
Hart VM *Balsall Heath – A History* Brewin Books (1992)
Hampson M *Images of England: Northfield Volume II* Tempus (2003)
Hemming A & Hart V *Britain in Old Photographs: Balsall Heath and Highgate Past and Present* Sutton (2003)
Moth J *The City of Birmingham Baths Department*

1851–1951 Birmingham City Council
Wilkins R *Turrets, Towels and Taps* Birmingham Museum and
Art Gallery (1984)
www.bclm.co.uk Black Country Living Museum

Chapter 18. Conclusions

DCMS *Protecting our Historic Environment: making the
system better* (2003)
ODPM *Planning Policy Guidance 17: Planning for open
space, sport and recreation* (2002)
Register of Historic Parks and Gardens
Register of Buildings at Risk

Periodicals and newspapers

Aris's Gazette; Birmingham Daily News; Birmingham Daily
Post; Birmingham Despatch; Birmingham Evening Mail;
Birmingham Gazette; Birmingham Post; Birmingham Post Year
Book and Who's Who; Birmingham Red Book and Reference
Almanac; Birmingham Sketch; Bournville Works Magazine;
Building Magazine; Cadbury News; Cornish's Birmingham
Yearbook; The Daily Telegraph; The Edgbastonia; Express
and Star; The Financial Times; Grass Roots; The Guardian;
Harborne Gazette; The Independent; Kelly's Directory of
Birmingham; Midland Chronicle for West Bromwich and
Oldbury; The Moorpool Duck; The Observer; Solihull News;
Solihull Times; Sport and Play; Sports Argus; Sutton Coldfield
Observer; The Times; Today; Wrighton's Directory

General reports

English Heritage *Power of Place: The Future of the Historic
Environment* (2002)
English Heritage *The State of England's Historic
Environment* (2005)
DCMS *The Historic Environment: A Force for our
Future* (2001)
Sport England/CABE *Better Places for Sport* (2003)

General websites

www.birminghamcivicsociety.org.uk
www.birmingham.gov.uk
www.birminghamsportscouncil.co.uk
www.culture.gov.uk
www.english-heritage.org.uk
www.imagesofengland.org.uk
www.lidos.org.uk
www.lookingatbuildings.org.uk
www.midlandspubs.co.uk
www.sandwell.gov.uk
www.savebritainsheritage.org
www.solihull.gov.uk
www.sportengland.org
www.virtualbrum.co.uk

Played in Britain

for more information on English
Heritage's *Played in Britain* series,
see www.playedinbritain.co.uk

Published titles

*Played in Manchester -
the architectural heritage of a city at
play* Simon Inglis *(2004)*

*Engineering Archie – Archibald Leitch,
football ground designer*
Simon Inglis *(2005)*

*Liquid Assets – the lidos and open air
swimming pools of Britain*
Janet Smith *(2005)*

A Load of Old Balls
Simon Inglis *(2005)*

Future titles

Played in Liverpool Ray Physick (2006)

*The Best of Charles Buchan Football
Monthly* ed. Simon Inglis (2006)

*Great Lengths – the indoor swimming
pools of Britain* Dr Ian Gordon (2007)

Played at the Pub Arthur Taylor (2007)

*Uppies & Downies – Britain's traditional
football games* Hugh Hornby (2007)

*Bowled Over – the bowling greens of
Britain* Hugh Hornby (2008)

Played in Glasgow Ged O'Brien (2008)

Played on Tyne & Wear Lynn Pearson
(date TBA)

Played in London Simon Inglis
(date TBA)

Credits

Photographs and images

Please note that in the credits below, where more than one photograph appears on a page, each photograph is identified by a letter, starting with 'a' in the top left hand corner of the page, or at the top, and continuing thereafter in a *clockwise* direction.

All English Heritage and National Monument Record photographs listed are © English Heritage or © Crown Copyright. NMR. Application for the reproduction of these images should be made to the National Monuments Record, at Kemble Drive, Swindon SN2 2GZ. Tel. 01793 414600.

All maps are Ordnance Survey © Crown Copyright

English Heritage/National Monuments Record photographs

James Davies: 6b, 34, 35bc, 36ab, 37b, 42a, 44b, 60a, 62ab, 63ab, 64bc, 65bc, 67ab, 84bcd, 90a, 106a, 108a, 110b, 118a, 121, 133ab, 138b, 140c, 142a, 152; Damian Grady: 15b, 16, 19, 24a, 26a, 38, 47, 50, 53, 58a, 61, 69a, 71a, 87a, 96, 99a, 110a, 117a, 133c; Derek Kendall: 23a, 24b, 39a, 82ab, 94b, 97c, 108b, 112b, 125b; National Monuments Record: 102ac

Commissioned photographs

Steve Beauchampé: 8, 66, 72c, 87b, 89a, 91a, 92b, 113b, 137c, 143b; Simon Inglis: cover flap, inside back cover, back cover abcd, 4, 6ac, 10b, 15a, 26b, 27a, 28ab, 39b, 41b, 46b, 51ac, 52a, 60b, 64a, 67c, 69b, 70a, 71b, 73b, 75bcd, 77, 86ab, 90b, 91b, 93, 94a, 97ab, 98bc, 99b, 101b, 106bc, 109, 112a, 113a, 114, 117cd, 122, 123, 124ab, 130a, 132, 134, 135, 136, 137ab, 139b, 142b, 143a, 144; Stephen McPhillips: 111

Archive photographs

Birmingham Central Library: 10a, 11a, 29, 48, 51b, 102b, 115 (reproduced with permission of Birmingham Botanical Gardens), 125a, 126b, 127b, 128, 129c, 130b, 131ab, 137d, 138a, 139a, 140abd, 141abcd; Birmingham Post & Mail: 2, 13ac, 14bc, 74ac, 88, 89b, 119, 120ab, 127a; National Portrait Gallery, London: 9; Sutton Coldfield Library: 57ab, 58bc, 59

Agency photographs

Colorsport: 11bc, 22ab, 23b, 49ab, 68abc, 70b, 73a, 98a, 145; Empics: 7; Getty Images: 1, 13b, 117b; NMPFT/Science & Society Picture Library: 105ac, 107b; NRM/Science &

Society Picture library: 42b; Simmons Aerofilms: 12, 43, 75a; Topfoto: 18, 25a, 116

Donated photographs

English Heritage would like to thank the following individuals and organisations for providing photographs and source material: Mike Bland: 78, 80ab, 84a, 85ab; Brooks England Ltd: 105b; Bryant Priest Newman/Rod Dorling: 25b; Cadbury Trebor Bassett: front cover, 30ab, 31, 32ab, 33, 35ad, 37a, 40; Edgbaston Golf Club: 27b; Thomas Fattorini Ltd: 101, 102d; Mike Frost: 65a; Joseph Hudson & Co: 100; Simon Inglis: 76a, 102b; Moseley Rugby Football Club: 72ab; Gordon Padmore: 107ac; Matt Pargeter: 92a; Chris Pitt: 56, 118b; Joan Preston: 129b; Bob Rowe: 44a, 74b; Roger Shayes: 46, 104; Solihull Barons: 126a; Trevor Starbuck: 151; John Wright: inside front cover, 14a, 52b, 54, 76b, 103, 129a

Acknowledgements

English Heritage and the authors would like to thank the many individuals, organisations and club representatives who assisted with information and research. They are especially grateful to Birmingham City Council for its sponsorship of the book, and in particular, Lorraine Mackay (Director of Marketing and Communications for the European Indoor Athletics Championships 2007) and Mike Dickenson (Partnerships Director at the Birmingham Sport and Physical Activity Partnership). At Birmingham Library Services, Peter Drake in Local Studies, David Bishop in Archives and Richard Albutt in the Digital Photographic Department were forever patient and efficient, as was Marian Baxter at Sutton Coldfield Reference Library. The staff of Yardley Wood and Hall Green District

Libraries and Solihull Library's Heritage and Local Studies Service were also extremely supportive. Further thanks go to Chris Smith, Nicholas Molyneux, Matt Dobson, Tim Johnston and Melanie Molloy at England Heritage West Midlands; to Rob Richardson and Dr René Rodgers at English Heritage Publications in Swindon; to Toni Demidowicz of Birmingham City Council's Conservation Group for her helpful comments on the text and for the additional contributions of her colleagues, and to Anna Burke in the *Birmingham Post and Mail* archive.

The following individuals were also generous with their time and knowledge: Fiona Adams (the Moseley Society), Roger Aitken and Anne Dawes (Edgbaston Priory Club), Anne Angell, Geoff Benson (Birmingham City Council), Ron Arkle (Rowheath Bowling Club), John Sharpe (Earlswood Town), Sue Bates, Naiomi Baumber (Bishop Challoner Sports Centre), Rod Bell (Bournville Cricket Club), Chris Bennett and Esther Jones (Edgbaston Croquet Club), Stuart Birch (King Edward's School), Michael Bland (Birmingham Works AFA), Paul Bloodworth (Woodcock Street Baths), Bob Boucher (Harborne Tenants Snooker Club), Colin Bowers (West Midlands Police), Phil Britt and Pasquale Norbury (Warwickshire CCC Museum), Robert Brooke, Don Brown (Brookvale & Sparkhill Sailing Club), Philip Calcutt, Keith Campbell, Steve Carr, Michael Cherry, Ken Baker and John Turner (Solihull Bowling Club), Harry Child, Carol Chown-Smith (Perry Barr Greyhound Stadium), Paul Clarke (Solihull School), Pastor Paul Clarke (Rowheath Pavilion), Dr Roy Cockel (Moseley Local History Society), Nigel Collins (Moor Green FC), Mike Colles (Midland Sailing Club), Jo Curtis (Birmingham Museum & Art Gallery), Damien Doran, Lee Downing (Hadley Stadium), Pat Eason, Susan J Elks and Chris Elks, Dorothy Fairfield (Woodlands Park Bowling Club), Greg and Tom Fattorini, Steve Fletcher (Northfield Baths), Dave Flora (Moseley Road Baths), Martin Florey and Gary Bruce (Portland Road Pavilions), Sarah Foden, Keith Tandy and Alan Beresford (Cadbury Trebor Bassett), Mike Frost and Pam Frost (Moor Pool Residents' Association), John Fry (British Roller Sports Federation), Bernard Gallagher, John Godfrey (Tally Ho! Bowling Club), Leon Goodchild, Adam Grint (Edgbaston Golf Club), Steve Harris (Munrow Sports Centre), Dr & Mrs Ahmed Hassam, Sam Hesketh (Edgbaston High School for Girls), William Hiscox and Harold Inglis (Shirley Golf Club), Bob Holland (Edgbaston Archery & Lawn Tennis Society), Stephen Howard, John Powell (Black Country Living Museum), Celia Hooper (Hallfield Preparatory School), Geoff Hunt (Ye Olde Knowle Bowling Club), Peter Jordan (Graingers), Adam Joyce (Billesley Community Fire Station), Graham Kidner (The Black Horse Bowls Club), Ken Lane (Solihull Blossomfield Sports Club), Anne Levitt (The Circle Tennis Club), Sue Lilleman (Moorpool Tennis Club), John Madin FRIBA, Neil Moore (Cadbury Social Club), Wilf Morgan (Birchfield Harriers), John Morton (Moseley Golf Club), Eileen Mulingarnie (Solihull Ice Rink), Clare Mullett (Collections Department, University of Birmingham), Mick O'Malley (Moorpool Skittles Club), Mike Osbourne (NEC Group), Gordon Padmore (Thurstons), Colin Peel, Chris Pitt (West Midlands Racing Club), Sheila Preece (Moorpool Air Rifle & Pistol Club), Joan Preston (Birmingham Ice Rink), Stephen Rea (GRA Ltd, Hall Green Stadium), Mick Roberts (Birmingham Wheels Park), Michael Ryan (Beechcroft Tennis Club), Roger Shayes (British Cycling Federation), Robin Shears (Moseley Ashfield CC), Keith Smart and Pete Davies (Birmingham Transport Stadium), Rachel Smith (Sparkhill Swimming Baths), Ann Stanton (Nechells Enterprise & Community Centre), Mark Stone (Moorpool Fishing Club), David Summerfield (Solihull Petanque Club), Scott and Craig Taylor (The Bell Inn Bowling Club), Christopher Thomas Architects, David Thompson (Sutton Coldfield Rifle & Small Bore Shooting Club), John Thorne (Avenue Bowling Club), Simon Topman (Hudson & Co), Geoff Tozer (Harborne Golf Club), Roger Unitt (Sutton Park Model Aero Club), Mike Wakelam (Warwickshire & Worcestershire Counties Bowling Association), Ken Watson (Kings Heath Archery Club), Joe Welch and Bob Nicholls (Moorpool Bowling Club), John Williams (Birmingham Anglers Association), John Whitehouse (Highgate United), Peter Woodrooffe (Moseley RFC) and Simon Wright (Grorty Dick fanzine).

Finally, the authors wish to express special thanks to Peggy and William Bousfield, to Alpesh, Sailesh and Preeti Chauhan, and to Harold, Wendy, Lynn and Theo Inglis, for their support and encouragement throughout.

After a dearth of quality sports architecture in Birmingham during the latter decades of the 20th century, there are clear signs of a new wave of buildings that express the spirit of the age no less admirably than many older examples celebrated in this book. The £1.65 million Bishop Challoner Sports Centre, Institute Road, King's Heath – by the Rush Davis Design Partnership – opened in 2004 and is used by Bishop Challoner School during the day, and by the community at evenings and weekends. A century earlier a facility like this would have hosted German or Swedish style gymnastics. Here there is a 'dojo', or training hall for Japanese martial arts.

Following page Classic Edwardian tilework and detailing at the oldest operational swimming pool in Birmingham – at Woodcock Street Baths, Gosta Green, first used in 1902.